T&p BOOKS

DICTIONARY
THEME–BASED

British English Collection

ENGLISH-
KOREAN

The most useful words
To expand your lexicon and sharpen
your language skills

3000 words

Theme-based dictionary British English-Korean - 3000 words
By Andrey Taranov

T&P Books vocabularies are intended for helping you learn, memorize and review foreign words. The dictionary is divided into themes, covering all major spheres of everyday activities, business, science, culture, etc.

The process of learning words using T&P Books' theme-based dictionaries gives you the following advantages:

- Correctly grouped source information predetermines success at subsequent stages of word memorization
- Availability of words derived from the same root allowing memorization of word units (rather than separate words)
- Small units of words facilitate the process of establishing associative links needed for consolidation of vocabulary
- Level of language knowledge can be estimated by the number of learned words

T&P Books Publishing
www.tpbooks.com

This book is also available in E-book formats.
Please visit www.tpbooks.com or the major online bookstores.

KOREAN THEME-BASED DICTIONARY
British English collection

T&P Books vocabularies are intended to help you learn, memorize, and review foreign words. The vocabulary contains over 3000 commonly used words arranged thematically.

- Vocabulary contains the most commonly used words
- Recommended as an addition to any language course
- Meets the needs of beginners and advanced learners of foreign languages
- Convenient for daily use, revision sessions, and self-testing activities
- Allows you to assess your vocabulary

Special features of the vocabulary

- Words are organized according to their meaning, not alphabetically
- Words are presented in three columns to facilitate the reviewing and self-testing processes
- Words in groups are divided into small blocks to facilitate the learning process
- The vocabulary offers a convenient and simple transcription of each foreign word

The vocabulary has 101 topics including:

Basic Concepts, Numbers, Colors, Months, Seasons, Units of Measurement, Clothing & Accessories, Food & Nutrition, Restaurant, Family Members, Relatives, Character, Feelings, Emotions, Diseases, City, Town, Sightseeing, Shopping, Money, House, Home, Office, Working in the Office, Import & Export, Marketing, Job Search, Sports, Education, Computer, Internet, Tools, Nature, Countries, Nationalities and more …

TABLE OF CONTENTS

PRONUNCIATION GUIDE

Letter	Korean example	T&P phonetic alphabet	English example
ㄱ [1]	개	[k]	clock, kiss
ㄱ [2]	아기	[g]	game, gold
ㄲ	껌	[k]	tense [k]
ㄴ	눈	[n]	name, normal
ㄷ [3]	달	[t]	tourist, trip
ㄷ [4]	사다리	[d]	day, doctor
ㄸ	딸	[t]	tense [t]
ㄹ [5]	라디오	[r]	rice, radio
ㄹ [6]	십팔	[l]	lace, people
ㅁ	문	[m]	magic, milk
ㅂ [7]	봄	[p]	pencil, private
ㅂ [8]	아버지	[b]	baby, book
ㅃ	빵	[p]	tense [p]
ㅅ [9]	실	[s]	city, boss
ㅅ [10]	옷	[t]	tourist, trip
ㅆ	쌀	[ja:]	royal
ㅇ [11]	강	[ŋg]	language, single
ㅈ [12]	집	[tɕ]	cheer
ㅈ [13]	아주	[dʑ]	jeans, gene
ㅉ	짬	[tɕ]	tense [tch]
ㅊ	차	[tʃh]	hitchhiker
ㅌ	택시	[th]	don't have
ㅋ	칼	[kh]	work hard
ㅍ	포도	[ph]	top hat
ㅎ	한국	[h]	home, have

Vowels and combinations with vowels

ㅏ	사	[a]	shorter than in 'ask'
ㅑ	향	[ja]	Kenya, piano
ㅓ	머리	[ʌ]	lucky, sun

Letter	Korean example	T&P phonetic alphabet	English example
ㅕ	병	[jɑ]	young, yard
ㅗ	몸	[o]	pod, John
ㅛ	표	[jɔ]	New York
ㅜ	물	[u]	book
ㅠ	슈퍼	[ju]	youth, usually
ㅡ	음악	[ɪ]	big, America
ㅣ	길	[i], [iː]	feet, Peter
ㅐ	뱀	[ɛ], [ɛː]	habit, bad
ㅒ	얘기	[je]	yesterday, yen
ㅔ	펜	[e]	elm, medal
ㅖ	계산	[je]	yesterday, yen
ㅘ	왕	[wa]	watt, white
ㅙ	왜	[ʊə]	pure, fuel
ㅚ	회의	[ø], [we]	first, web
ㅝ	권	[uɔ]	to order, to open
ㅞ	웬	[ʊə]	pure, fuel
ㅟ	쥐	[wi]	whiskey
ㅢ	거의	[ɯi]	combination [ɪi]

Comments

[1] at the beginning of words
[2] between voiced sounds
[3] at the beginning of words
[4] between voiced sounds
[5] at the beginning of a syllable
[6] at the end of a syllable
[7] at the beginning of words
[8] between voiced sounds
[9] at the beginning of a syllable
[10] at the end of a syllable
[11] at the end of a syllable
[12] at the beginning of words
[13] between voiced sounds

ABBREVIATIONS
used in the dictionary

English abbreviations

ab.	-	about
adj	-	adjective
adv	-	adverb
anim.	-	animate
as adj	-	attributive noun used as adjective
e.g.	-	for example
etc.	-	et cetera
fam.	-	familiar
fem.	-	feminine
form.	-	formal
inanim.	-	inanimate
masc.	-	masculine
math	-	mathematics
mil.	-	military
n	-	noun
pl	-	plural
pron.	-	pronoun
sb	-	somebody
sing.	-	singular
sth	-	something
v aux	-	auxiliary verb
vi	-	intransitive verb
vi, vt	-	intransitive, transitive verb
vt	-	transitive verb

BASIC CONCEPTS

1. Pronouns

I, me	나, 저	na
you	너	neo
he	그, 그분	geu, geu-bun
she	그녀	geu-nyeo
it	그것	geu-geot
we	우리	u-ri
you (to a group)	너희	neo-hui
you (polite, sing.)	당신	dang-sin
they	그들	geu-deul

2. Greetings. Salutations

Hello! (fam.)	안녕!	an-nyeong!
Hello! (form.)	안녕하세요!	an-nyeong-ha-se-yo!
Good morning!	안녕하세요!	an-nyeong-ha-se-yo!
Good afternoon!	안녕하세요!	an-nyeong-ha-se-yo!
Good evening!	안녕하세요!	an-nyeong-ha-se-yo!
to say hello	인사하다	in-sa-ha-da
Hi! (hello)	안녕!	an-nyeong!
greeting (n)	인사	in-sa
to greet (vt)	인사하다	in-sa-ha-da
How are you?	잘 지내세요?	jal ji-nae-se-yo?
What's new?	어떻게 지내?	eo-tteo-ke ji-nae?
Bye-Bye! Goodbye!	안녕히 가세요!	an-nyeong-hi ga-se-yo!
See you soon!	또 만나요!	tto man-na-yo!
Farewell! (to a friend)	잘 있어!	jal ri-seo!
Farewell! (form.)	안녕히 계세요!	an-nyeong-hi gye-se-yo!
to say goodbye	작별인사를 하다	jak-byeo-rin-sa-reul ha-da
Cheers!	안녕!	an-nyeong!
Thank you! Cheers!	감사합니다!	gam-sa-ham-ni-da!
Thank you very much!	대단히 감사합니다!	dae-dan-hi gam-sa-ham-ni-da!
My pleasure!	천만이에요	cheon-man-i-e-yo
Don't mention it!	천만의 말씀입니다	cheon-man-ui mal-sseum-im-ni-da
It was nothing	천만에	cheon-man-e
Excuse me! (fam.)	실례!	sil-lye!
Excuse me! (form.)	실례합니다!	sil-lye-ham-ni-da!

to excuse (forgive)	용서하다	yong-seo-ha-da
to apologize (vi)	사과하다	sa-gwa-ha-da
My apologies	사과드립니다	sa-gwa-deu-rim-ni-da
I'm sorry!	죄송합니다!	joe-song-ham-ni-da!
to forgive (vt)	용서하다	yong-seo-ha-da
please (adv)	부탁합니다	bu-tak-am-ni-da
Don't forget!	잊지 마십시오!	it-ji ma-sip-si-o!
Certainly!	물론이에요!	mul-lon-i-e-yo!
Of course not!	물론 아니에요!	mul-lon a-ni-e-yo!
Okay! (I agree)	그래요!	geu-rae-yo!
That's enough!	그만!	geu-man!

3. Questions

Who?	누구?	nu-gu?
What?	무엇?	mu-eot?
Where? (at, in)	어디?	eo-di?
Where (to)?	어디로?	eo-di-ro?
From where?	어디로부터?	eo-di-ro-bu-teo?
When?	언제?	eon-je?
Why? (What for?)	왜?	wae?
Why? (~ are you crying?)	왜?	wae?
What for?	무엇을 위해서?	mu-eos-eul rwi-hae-seo?
How? (in what way)	어떻게?	eo-tteo-ke?
What? (What kind of ...?)	어떤?	eo-tteon?
Which?	어느?	eo-neu?
To whom?	누구에게?	nu-gu-e-ge?
About whom?	누구에 대하여?	nu-gu-e dae-ha-yeo?
About what?	무엇에 대하여?	mu-eos-e dae-ha-yeo?
With whom?	누구하고?	nu-gu-ha-go?
How many? How much?	얼마?	eol-ma?
Whose?	누구의?	nu-gu-ui?

4. Prepositions

with (accompanied by)	⋯ 하고	... ha-go
without	없이	eop-si
to (indicating direction)	⋯ 에	... e
about (talking ~ ...)	⋯ 에 대하여	... e dae-ha-yeo
before (in time)	전에	jeon-e
in front of ...	⋯ 앞에	... a-pe
under (beneath, below)	밑에	mi-te
above (over)	위에	wi-e
on (atop)	위에	wi-e
from (off, out of)	⋯ 에서	... e-seo
of (made from)	⋯ 로	... ro
in (e.g. ~ ten minutes)	⋯ 안에	... a-ne
over (across the top of)	너머	dwi-e

5. Function words. Adverbs. Part 1

Where? (at, in)	어디?	eo-di?
here (adv)	여기	yeo-gi
there (adv)	거기	geo-gi
somewhere (to be)	어딘가	eo-din-ga
nowhere (not in any place)	어디도	eo-di-do
by (near, beside)	옆에	yeo-pe
by the window	창문 옆에	chang-mun nyeo-pe
Where (to)?	어디로?	eo-di-ro?
here (e.g. come ~!)	여기로	yeo-gi-ro
there (e.g. to go ~)	거기로	geo-gi-ro
from here (adv)	여기서	yeo-gi-seo
from there (adv)	거기서	geo-gi-seo
close (adv)	가까이	ga-kka-i
far (adv)	멀리	meol-li
near (e.g. ~ Paris)	근처에	geun-cheo-e
nearby (adv)	인근에	in-geu-ne
not far (adv)	멀지 않게	meol-ji an-ke
left (adj)	왼쪽의	oen-jjo-gui
on the left	왼쪽에	oen-jjo-ge
to the left	왼쪽으로	oen-jjo-geu-ro
right (adj)	오른쪽의	o-reun-jjo-gui
on the right	오른쪽에	o-reun-jjo-ge
to the right	오른쪽으로	o-reun-jjo-geu-ro
in front (adv)	앞쪽에	ap-jjo-ge
front (as adj)	앞의	a-pui
ahead (the kids ran ~)	앞으로	a-peu-ro
behind (adv)	뒤에	dwi-e
from behind	뒤에서	dwi-e-seo
back (towards the rear)	뒤로	dwi-ro
middle	가운데	ga-un-de
in the middle	가운데에	ga-un-de-e
at the side	옆에	yeo-pe
everywhere (adv)	모든 곳에	mo-deun gos-e
around (in all directions)	주위에	ju-wi-e
from inside	내면에서	nae-myeon-e-seo
somewhere (to go)	어딘가에	eo-din-ga-e
straight (directly)	똑바로	ttok-ba-ro
back (e.g. come ~)	뒤로	dwi-ro
from anywhere	어디에서든지	eo-di-e-seo-deun-ji
from somewhere	어디로부터인지	eo-di-ro-bu-teo-in-ji

firstly (adv)	첫째로	cheot-jjae-ro
secondly (adv)	둘째로	dul-jjae-ro
thirdly (adv)	셋째로	set-jjae-ro
suddenly (adv)	갑자기	gap-ja-gi
at first (in the beginning)	처음에	cheo-eum-e
for the first time	처음으로	cheo-eu-meu-ro
long before ...	··· 오래 전에	... o-rae jeon-e
anew (over again)	다시	da-si
for good (adv)	영원히	yeong-won-hi
never (adv)	절대로	jeol-dae-ro
again (adv)	다시	da-si
now (at present)	이제	i-je
often (adv)	자주	ja-ju
then (adv)	그때	geu-ttae
urgently (quickly)	급히	geu-pi
usually (adv)	보통으로	bo-tong-eu-ro
by the way, ...	그건 그렇고, ···	geu-geon geu-reo-ko, ...
possibly	가능한	ga-neung-han
probably (adv)	아마	a-ma
maybe (adv)	어쩌면	eo-jjeo-myeon
besides ...	게다가 ···	ge-da-ga ...
that's why ...	그래서 ···	geu-rae-seo ...
in spite of ...	··· 에도 불구하고	... e-do bul-gu-ha-go
thanks to ...	··· 덕분에	... deok-bun-e
something	무엇인가	mu-eon-nin-ga
anything (something)	무엇이든지	mu-eon-ni-deun-ji
nothing	아무것도	a-mu-geot-do
someone	누구	nu-gu
somebody	누군가	nu-gun-ga
nobody	아무도	a-mu-do
nowhere (a voyage to ~)	아무데도	a-mu-de-do
nobody's	누구의 것도 아닌	nu-gu-ui geot-do a-nin
somebody's	누군가의	nu-gun-ga-ui
so (I'm ~ glad)	그래서	geu-rae-seo
also (as well)	역시	yeok-si
too (as well)	또한	tto-han

6. Function words. Adverbs. Part 2

Why?	왜?	wae?
for some reason	어떤 이유로	eo-tteon ni-yu-ro
because ...	왜냐하면 ···	wae-nya-ha-myeon ...
for some purpose	어떤 목적으로	eo-tteon mok-jeo-geu-ro
and	그리고	geu-ri-go
or	또는	tto-neun
but	그러나	geu-reo-na

for (e.g. ~ me)	위해서	wi-hae-seo
too (excessively)	너무	neo-mu
only (exclusively)	··· 만	... man
exactly (adv)	정확하게	jeong-hwak-a-ge
about (more or less)	약	yak
approximately (adv)	대략	dae-ryak
approximate (adj)	대략적인	dae-ryak-jeo-gin
almost (adv)	거의	geo-ui
the rest	나머지	na-meo-ji
each (adj)	각각의	gak-ga-gui
any (no matter which)	아무	a-mu
many, much (a lot of)	많이	ma-ni
many people	많은 사람들	ma-neun sa-ram-deul
all (everyone)	모두	mo-du
in return for ...	··· 의 교환으로	... ui gyo-hwa-neu-ro
in exchange (adv)	교환으로	gyo-hwa-neu-ro
by hand (made)	수공으로	su-gong-eu-ro
hardly (negative opinion)	거의	geo-ui
probably (adv)	아마	a-ma
on purpose (intentionally)	일부러	il-bu-reo
by accident (adv)	우연히	u-yeon-hi
very (adv)	아주	a-ju
for example (adv)	예를 들면	ye-reul deul-myeon
between	사이에	sa-i-e
among	중에	jung-e
so much (such a lot)	이만큼	i-man-keum
especially (adv)	특히	teuk-i

NUMBERS. MISCELLANEOUS

7. Cardinal numbers. Part 1

0 zero	영	yeong
1 one	일	il
2 two	이	i
3 three	삼	sam
4 four	사	sa
5 five	오	o
6 six	육	yuk
7 seven	칠	chil
8 eight	팔	pal
9 nine	구	gu
10 ten	십	sip
11 eleven	십일	si-bil
12 twelve	십이	si-bi
13 thirteen	십삼	sip-sam
14 fourteen	십사	sip-sa
15 fifteen	십오	si-bo
16 sixteen	십육	si-byuk
17 seventeen	십칠	sip-chil
18 eighteen	십팔	sip-pal
19 nineteen	십구	sip-gu
20 twenty	이십	i-sip
21 twenty-one	이십일	i-si-bil
22 twenty-two	이십이	i-si-bi
23 twenty-three	이십삼	i-sip-sam
30 thirty	삼십	sam-sip
31 thirty-one	삼십일	sam-si-bil
32 thirty-two	삼십이	sam-si-bi
33 thirty-three	삼십삼	sam-sip-sam
40 forty	사십	sa-sip
41 forty-one	사십일	sa-si-bil
42 forty-two	사십이	sa-si-bi
43 forty-three	사십삼	sa-sip-sam
50 fifty	오십	o-sip
51 fifty-one	오십일	o-si-bil
52 fifty-two	오십이	o-si-bi
53 fifty-three	오십삼	o-sip-sam
60 sixty	육십	yuk-sip
61 sixty-one	육십일	yuk-si-bil

| 62 sixty-two | 육십이 | yuk-si-bi |
| 63 sixty-three | 육십삼 | yuk-sip-sam |

70 seventy	칠십	chil-sip
71 seventy-one	칠십일	chil-si-bil
72 seventy-two	칠십이	chil-si-bi
73 seventy-three	칠십삼	chil-sip-sam

80 eighty	팔십	pal-sip
81 eighty-one	팔십일	pal-si-bil
82 eighty-two	팔십이	pal-si-bi
83 eighty-three	팔십삼	pal-sip-sam

90 ninety	구십	gu-sip
91 ninety-one	구십일	gu-si-bil
92 ninety-two	구십이	gu-si-bi
93 ninety-three	구십삼	gu-sip-sam

8. Cardinal numbers. Part 2

100 one hundred	백	baek
200 two hundred	이백	i-baek
300 three hundred	삼백	sam-baek
400 four hundred	사백	sa-baek
500 five hundred	오백	o-baek

600 six hundred	육백	yuk-baek
700 seven hundred	칠백	chil-baek
800 eight hundred	팔백	pal-baek
900 nine hundred	구백	gu-baek

1000 one thousand	천	cheon
2000 two thousand	이천	i-cheon
3000 three thousand	삼천	sam-cheon
10000 ten thousand	만	man
one hundred thousand	십만	sim-man
million	백만	baeng-man
billion	십억	si-beok

9. Ordinal numbers

first (adj)	첫 번째의	cheot beon-jjae-ui
second (adj)	두 번째의	du beon-jjae-ui
third (adj)	세 번째의	se beon-jjae-ui
fourth (adj)	네 번째의	ne beon-jjae-ui
fifth (adj)	다섯 번째의	da-seot beon-jjae-ui

sixth (adj)	여섯 번째의	yeo-seot beon-jjae-ui
seventh (adj)	일곱 번째의	il-gop beon-jjae-ui
eighth (adj)	여덟 번째의	yeo-deol beon-jjae-ui
ninth (adj)	아홉 번째의	a-hop beon-jjae-ui
tenth (adj)	열 번째의	yeol beon-jjae-ui

COLORS. UNITS OF MEASUREMENT

10. Colours

colour	색	sae
shade (tint)	색조	saek-jo
hue	색상	saek-sang
rainbow	무지개	mu-ji-gae
white (adj)	흰	huin
black (adj)	검은	geo-meun
grey (adj)	회색의	hoe-sae-gui
green (adj)	초록색의	cho-rok-sae-gui
yellow (adj)	노란	no-ran
red (adj)	빨간	ppal-gan
blue (adj)	파란	pa-ran
light blue (adj)	하늘색의	ha-neul-sae-gui
pink (adj)	분홍색의	bun-hong-sae-gui
orange (adj)	주황색의	ju-hwang-sae-gui
violet (adj)	보라색의	bo-ra-sae-gui
brown (adj)	갈색의	gal-sae-gui
golden (adj)	금색의	geum-sae-gui
silvery (adj)	은색의	eun-sae-gui
beige (adj)	베이지색의	be-i-ji-sae-gui
cream (adj)	크림색의	keu-rim-sae-gui
turquoise (adj)	청록색의	cheong-nok-sae-gui
cherry red (adj)	암적색의	am-jeok-sae-gui
lilac (adj)	연보라색의	yeon-bo-ra-sae-gui
crimson (adj)	진홍색의	jin-hong-sae-gui
light (adj)	밝은	bal-geun
dark (adj)	짙은	ji-teun
bright, vivid (adj)	선명한	seon-myeong-han
coloured (pencils)	색의	sae-gui
colour (e.g. ~ film)	컬러의	keol-leo-ui
black-and-white (adj)	흑백의	heuk-bae-gui
plain (one-coloured)	단색의	dan-sae-gui
multicoloured (adj)	다색의	da-sae-gui

11. Units of measurement

weight	무게	mu-ge
length	길이	gi-ri

width	폭, 너비	pok, neo-bi
height	높이	no-pi
depth	깊이	gi-pi
volume	부피	bu-pi
area	면적	myeon-jeok
gram	그램	geu-raem
milligram	밀리그램	mil-li-geu-raem
kilogram	킬로그램	kil-lo-geu-raem
ton	톤	ton
pound	파운드	pa-un-deu
ounce	온스	on-seu
metre	미터	mi-teo
millimetre	밀리미터	mil-li-mi-teo
centimetre	센티미터	sen-ti-mi-teo
kilometre	킬로미터	kil-lo-mi-teo
mile	마일	ma-il
inch	인치	in-chi
foot	피트	pi-teu
yard	야드	ya-deu
square metre	제곱미터	je-gom-mi-teo
hectare	헥타르	hek-ta-reu
litre	리터	ri-teo
degree	도	do
volt	볼트	bol-teu
ampere	암페어	am-pe-eo
horsepower	마력	ma-ryeok
quantity	수량, 양	su-ryang, yang
a little bit of ...	... 조금	... jo-geum
half	절반	jeol-ban
dozen	다스	da-seu
piece (item)	조각	jo-gak
size	크기	keu-gi
scale (map ~)	축척	chuk-cheok
minimal (adj)	최소의	choe-so-ui
the smallest (adj)	가장 작은	ga-jang ja-geun
medium (adj)	중간의	jung-gan-ui
maximal (adj)	최대의	choe-dae-ui
the largest (adj)	가장 큰	ga-jang keun

12. Containers

canning jar (glass ~)	유리병	yu-ri-byeong
tin, can	캔, 깡통	kaen, kkang-tong
bucket	양동이	yang-dong-i
barrel	통	tong
wash basin (e.g., plastic ~)	대야	dae-ya

tank (100L water ~)	탱크	taeng-keu
hip flask	휴대용 술병	hyu-dae-yong sul-byeong
jerrycan	통	tong
tank (e.g., tank car)	탱크	taeng-keu
mug	머그컵	meo-geu-keop
cup (of coffee, etc.)	컵	keop
saucer	받침 접시	bat-chim jeop-si
glass (tumbler)	유리잔	yu-ri-jan
wine glass	와인글라스	wa-in-geul-la-seu
stock pot (soup pot)	냄비	naem-bi
bottle (~ of wine)	병	byeong
neck (of the bottle, etc.)	병목	byeong-mok
carafe (decanter)	디캔터	di-kaen-teo
pitcher	물병	mul-byeong
vessel (container)	용기	yong-gi
pot (crock, stoneware ~)	항아리	hang-a-ri
vase	화병	hwa-byeong
flacon, bottle (perfume ~)	향수병	hyang-su-byeong
vial, small bottle	약병	yak-byeong
tube (of toothpaste)	튜브	tyu-beu
sack (bag)	자루	ja-ru
bag (paper ~, plastic ~)	봉투	bong-tu
packet (of cigarettes, etc.)	갑	gap
box (e.g. shoebox)	박스	bak-seu
crate	상자	sang-ja
basket	바구니	ba-gu-ni

MAIN VERBS

13. The most important verbs. Part 1

to advise (vt)	조언하다	jo-eon-ha-da
to agree (say yes)	동의하다	dong-ui-ha-da
to answer (vi, vt)	대답하다	dae-da-pa-da
to apologize (vi)	사과하다	sa-gwa-ha-da
to arrive (vi)	도착하다	do-chak-a-da
to ask (~ oneself)	묻다	mut-da
to ask (~ sb to do sth)	부탁하다	bu-tak-a-da
to be afraid	무서워하다	mu-seo-wo-ha-da
to be hungry	배가 고프다	bae-ga go-peu-da
to be interested in ...	··· 에 관심을 가지다	... e gwan-si-meul ga-ji-da
to be needed	필요하다	pi-ryo-ha-da
to be surprised	놀라다	nol-la-da
to be thirsty	목마르다	mong-ma-reu-da
to begin (vt)	시작하다	si-jak-a-da
to belong to ...	··· 에 속하다	... e sok-a-da
to boast (vi)	자랑하다	ja-rang-ha-da
to break (split into pieces)	깨뜨리다	kkae-tteu-ri-da
to call (~ for help)	부르다, 요청하다	bu-reu-da, yo-cheong-ha-da
can (v aux)	할 수 있다	hal su it-da
to catch (vt)	잡다	jap-da
to change (vt)	바꾸다	ba-kku-da
to choose (select)	선택하다	seon-taek-a-da
to come down (the stairs)	내려오다	nae-ryeo-o-da
to compare (vt)	비교하다	bi-gyo-ha-da
to complain (vi, vt)	불평하다	bul-pyeong-ha-da
to confuse (mix up)	혼동하다	hon-dong-ha-da
to continue (vt)	계속하다	gye-sok-a-da
to control (vt)	제어하다	je-eo-ha-da
to cook (dinner)	요리하다	yo-ri-ha-da
to cost (vt)	값이 ··· 이다	gap-si ... i-da
to count (add up)	세다	se-da
to count on ...	··· 에 의지하다	... e ui-ji-ha-da
to create (vt)	창조하다	chang-jo-ha-da
to cry (weep)	울다	ul-da

14. The most important verbs. Part 2

to deceive (vi, vt)	속이다	so-gi-da
to decorate (tree, street)	장식하다	jang-sik-a-da

to defend (a country, etc.)	방어하다	bang-eo-ha-da
to demand (request firmly)	요구하다	yo-gu-ha-da
to dig (vt)	파다	pa-da
to discuss (vt)	의논하다	ui-non ha-da
to do (vt)	하다	ha-da
to doubt (have doubts)	의심하다	ui-sim-ha-da
to drop (let fall)	떨어뜨리다	tteo-reo-tteu-ri-da
to enter (room, house, etc.)	들어가다	deu-reo-ga-da
to exist (vi)	존재하다	jon-jae-ha-da
to expect (foresee)	예상하다	ye-sang-ha-da
to explain (vt)	설명하다	seol-myeong-ha-da
to fall (vi)	떨어지다	tteo-reo-ji-da
to fancy (vt)	좋아하다	jo-a-ha-da
to find (vt)	찾다	chat-da
to finish (vt)	끝내다	kkeun-nae-da
to fly (vi)	날다	nal-da
to follow ... (come after)	··· 를 따라가다	... reul tta-ra-ga-da
to forget (vi, vt)	잊다	it-da
to forgive (vt)	용서하다	yong-seo-ha-da
to give (vt)	주다	ju-da
to give a hint	힌트를 주다	hin-teu-reul ju-da
to go (on foot)	가다	ga-da
to go for a swim	수영하다	su-yeong-ha-da
to go out (for dinner, etc.)	나가다	na-ga-da
to guess (the answer)	추측하다	chu-cheuk-a-da
to have (vt)	가지다	ga-ji-da
to have breakfast	아침을 먹다	a-chi-meul meok-da
to have dinner	저녁을 먹다	jeo-nyeo-geul meok-da
to have lunch	점심을 먹다	jeom-si-meul meok-da
to hear (vt)	듣다	deut-da
to help (vt)	도와주다	do-wa-ju-da
to hide (vt)	숨기다	sum-gi-da
to hope (vi, vt)	희망하다	hui-mang-ha-da
to hunt (vi, vt)	사냥하다	sa-nyang-ha-da
to hurry (vi)	서두르다	seo-du-reu-da

15. The most important verbs. Part 3

to inform (vt)	알리다	al-li-da
to insist (vi, vt)	주장하다	ju-jang-ha-da
to insult (vt)	모욕하다	mo-yok-a-da
to invite (vt)	초대하다	cho-dae-ha-da
to joke (vi)	농담하다	nong-dam-ha-da
to keep (vt)	보관하다	bo-gwan-ha-da
to keep silent, to hush	침묵을 지키다	chim-mu-geul ji-ki-da
to kill (vt)	죽이다	ju-gi-da

to know (sb)	알다	al-da
to know (sth)	알다	al-da
to laugh (vi)	웃다	ut-da

to liberate (city, etc.)	해방하다	hae-bang-ha-da
to look for … (search)	… 를 찾다	… reul chat-da
to love (sb)	사랑하다	sa-rang-ha-da
to make a mistake	실수하다	sil-su-ha-da
to manage, to run	운영하다	u-nyeong-ha-da

to mean (signify)	의미하다	ui-mi-ha-da
to mention (talk about)	언급하다	eon-geu-pa-da
to miss (school, etc.)	결석하다	gyeol-seok-a-da
to notice (see)	알아차리다	a-ra-cha-ri-da
to object (vi, vt)	반대하다	ban-dae-ha-da

to observe (see)	지켜보다	ji-kyeo-bo-da
to open (vt)	열다	yeol-da
to order (meal, etc.)	주문하다	ju-mun-ha-da
to order (mil.)	명령하다	myeong-nyeong-ha-da
to own (possess)	소유하다	so-yu-ha-da

to participate (vi)	참가하다	cham-ga-ha-da
to pay (vi, vt)	지불하다	ji-bul-ha-da
to permit (vt)	허가하다	heo-ga-ha-da
to plan (vt)	계획하다	gye-hoek-a-da
to play (children)	놀다	nol-da

to pray (vi, vt)	기도하다	gi-do-ha-da
to prefer (vt)	선호하다	seon-ho-ha-da
to promise (vt)	약속하다	yak-sok-a-da
to pronounce (vt)	발음하다	ba-reum-ha-da
to propose (vt)	제안하다	je-an-ha-da
to punish (vt)	처벌하다	cheo-beol-ha-da

16. The most important verbs. Part 4

to read (vi, vt)	읽다	ik-da
to recommend (vt)	추천하다	chu-cheon-ha-da
to refuse (vi, vt)	거절하다	geo-jeol-ha-da
to regret (be sorry)	후회하다	hu-hoe-ha-da
to rent (sth from sb)	임대하다	im-dae-ha-da

to repeat (say again)	반복하다	ban-bok-a-da
to reserve, to book	예약하다	ye-yak-a-da
to run (vi)	달리다	dal-li-da
to save (rescue)	구조하다	gu-jo-ha-da

to say (~ thank you)	말하다	mal-ha-da
to scold (vt)	꾸짖다	kku-jit-da
to see (vt)	보다	bo-da
to sell (vt)	팔다	pal-da
to send (vt)	보내다	bo-nae-da
to shoot (vi)	쏘다	sso-da

to shout (vi)	소리치다	so-ri-chi-da
to show (vt)	보여주다	bo-yeo-ju-da
to sign (document)	서명하다	seo-myeong-ha-da
to sit down (vi)	앉다	an-da
to smile (vi)	미소를 짓다	mi-so-reul jit-da
to speak (vi, vt)	말하다	mal-ha-da
to steal (money, etc.)	훔치다	hum-chi-da
to stop (for pause, etc.)	정지하다	jeong-ji-ha-da
to stop (please ~ calling me)	그만두다	geu-man-du-da
to study (vt)	공부하다	gong-bu-ha-da
to swim (vi)	수영하다	su-yeong-ha-da
to take (vt)	잡다	jap-da
to think (vi, vt)	생각하다	saeng-gak-a-da
to threaten (vt)	협박하다	hyeop-bak-a-da
to touch (with hands)	닿다	da-ta
to translate (vt)	번역하다	beo-nyeok-a-da
to trust (vt)	신뢰하다	sil-loe-ha-da
to try (attempt)	해보다	hae-bo-da
to turn (e.g., ~ left)	돌다	dol-da
to underestimate (vt)	과소평가하다	gwa-so-pyeong-ga-ha-da
to understand (vt)	이해하다	i-hae-ha-da
to unite (vt)	연합하다	yeon-ha-pa-da
to wait (vt)	기다리다	gi-da-ri-da
to want (wish, desire)	원하다	won-ha-da
to warn (vt)	경고하다	gyeong-go-ha-da
to work (vi)	일하다	il-ha-da
to write (vt)	쓰다	sseu-da
to write down	적다	jeok-da

TIME. CALENDAR

17. Weekdays

Monday	월요일	wo-ryo-il
Tuesday	화요일	hwa-yo-il
Wednesday	수요일	su-yo-il
Thursday	목요일	mo-gyo-il
Friday	금요일	geu-myo-il
Saturday	토요일	to-yo-il
Sunday	일요일	i-ryo-il
today (adv)	오늘	o-neul
tomorrow (adv)	내일	nae-il
the day after tomorrow	모레	mo-re
yesterday (adv)	어제	eo-je
the day before yesterday	그저께	geu-jeo-kke
day	낮	nat
working day	근무일	geun-mu-il
public holiday	공휴일	gong-hyu-il
day off	휴일	hyu-il
weekend	주말	ju-mal
all day long	하루종일	ha-ru-jong-il
the next day (adv)	다음날	da-eum-nal
two days ago	이틀 전	i-teul jeon
the day before	전날	jeon-nal
daily (adj)	일간의	il-ga-nui
every day (adv)	매일	mae-il
week	주	ju
last week (adv)	지난 주에	ji-nan ju-e
next week (adv)	다음 주에	da-eum ju-e
weekly (adj)	주간의	ju-ga-nui
every week (adv)	매주	mae-ju
twice a week	일주일에 두번	il-ju-i-re du-beon
every Tuesday	매주 화요일	mae-ju hwa-yo-il

18. Hours. Day and night

morning	아침	a-chim
in the morning	아침에	a-chim-e
noon, midday	정오	jeong-o
in the afternoon	오후에	o-hu-e
evening	저녁	jeo-nyeok
in the evening	저녁에	jeo-nyeo-ge

night	밤	bam
at night	밤에	bam-e
midnight	자정	ja-jeong
second	초	cho
minute	분	bun
hour	시	si
half an hour	반시간	ban-si-gan
a quarter-hour	십오분	si-bo-bun
fifteen minutes	십오분	si-bo-bun
24 hours	이십사시간	i-sip-sa-si-gan
sunrise	일출	il-chul
dawn	새벽	sae-byeok
early morning	이른 아침	i-reun a-chim
sunset	저녁 노을	jeo-nyeok no-eul
early in the morning	이른 아침에	i-reun a-chim-e
this morning	오늘 아침에	o-neul ra-chim-e
tomorrow morning	내일 아침에	nae-il ra-chim-e
this afternoon	오늘 오후에	o-neul ro-hu-e
in the afternoon	오후에	o-hu-e
tomorrow afternoon	내일 오후에	nae-il ro-hu-e
tonight (this evening)	오늘 저녁에	o-neul jeo-nyeo-ge
tomorrow night	내일 밤에	nae-il bam-e
at 3 o'clock sharp	3시 정각에	se-si jeong-ga-ge
about 4 o'clock	4시쯤에	ne-si-jjeu-me
by 12 o'clock	12시까지	yeoldu si-kka-ji
in 20 minutes	20분 안에	isib-bun na-ne
in an hour	한 시간 안에	han si-gan na-ne
on time (adv)	제시간에	je-si-gan-e
a quarter to ...	··· 십오 분	... si-bo bun
within an hour	한 시간 내에	han si-gan nae-e
every 15 minutes	15분 마다	sibo-bun ma-da
round the clock	하루종일	ha-ru-jong-il

19. Months. Seasons

January	일월	i-rwol
February	이월	i-wol
March	삼월	sam-wol
April	사월	sa-wol
May	오월	o-wol
June	유월	yu-wol
July	칠월	chi-rwol
August	팔월	pa-rwol
September	구월	gu-wol
October	시월	si-wol

| November | 십일월 | si-bi-rwol |
| December | 십이월 | si-bi-wol |

spring	봄	bom
in spring	봄에	bom-e
spring (as adj)	봄의	bom-ui

summer	여름	yeo-reum
in summer	여름에	yeo-reum-e
summer (as adj)	여름의	yeo-reu-mui

autumn	가을	ga-eul
in autumn	가을에	ga-eu-re
autumn (as adj)	가을의	ga-eu-rui

winter	겨울	gyeo-ul
in winter	겨울에	gyeo-u-re
winter (as adj)	겨울의	gyeo-ul

month	월, 달	wol, dal
this month	이번 달에	i-beon da-re
next month	다음 달에	da-eum da-re
last month	지난 달에	ji-nan da-re

a month ago	한달 전에	han-dal jeon-e
in a month (a month later)	한 달 안에	han dal ra-ne
in 2 months (2 months later)	두 달 안에	du dal ra-ne
the whole month	한 달 내내	han dal lae-nae
all month long	한달간 내내	han-dal-gan nae-nae

monthly (~ magazine)	월간의	wol-ga-nui
monthly (adv)	매월, 매달	mae-wol, mae-dal
every month	매달	mae-dal
twice a month	한 달에 두 번	han da-re du beon

year	년	nyeon
this year	올해	ol-hae
next year	내년	nae-nyeon
last year	작년	jang-nyeon

a year ago	일년 전	il-lyeon jeon
in a year	일 년 안에	il lyeon na-ne
in two years	이 년 안에	i nyeon na-ne
the whole year	한 해 전체	han hae jeon-che
all year long	일년 내내	il-lyeon nae-nae

every year	매년	mae-nyeon
annual (adj)	연간의	yeon-ga-nui
annually (adv)	매년	mae-nyeon
4 times a year	일년에 네 번	il-lyeon-e ne beon

date (e.g. today's ~)	날짜	nal-jja
date (e.g. ~ of birth)	월일	wo-ril
calendar	달력	dal-lyeok
half a year	반년	ban-nyeon
six months	육개월	yuk-gae-wol

| season (summer, etc.) | 계절 | gye-jeol |
| century | 세기 | se-gi |

TRAVEL. HOTEL

20. Trip. Travel

tourism, travel	관광	gwan-gwang
tourist	관광객	gwan-gwang-gaek
trip, voyage	여행	yeo-haeng
adventure	모험	mo-heom
trip, journey	여행	yeo-haeng
holiday	휴가	hyu-ga
to be on holiday	휴가 중이다	hyu-ga jung-i-da
rest	휴양	hyu-yang
train	기차	gi-cha
by train	기차로	gi-cha-ro
aeroplane	비행기	bi-haeng-gi
by aeroplane	비행기로	bi-haeng-gi-ro
by car	자동차로	ja-dong-cha-ro
by ship	배로	bae-ro
luggage	짐, 수하물	jim, su-ha-mul
suitcase	여행 가방	yeo-haeng ga-bang
luggage trolley	수하물 카트	su-ha-mul ka-teu
passport	여권	yeo-gwon
visa	비자	bi-ja
ticket	표	pyo
air ticket	비행기표	bi-haeng-gi-pyo
guidebook	여행 안내서	yeo-haeng an-nae-seo
map (tourist ~)	지도	ji-do
area (rural ~)	지역	ji-yeok
place, site	곳	got
exotica (n)	이국	i-guk
exotic (adj)	이국적인	i-guk-jeo-gin
amazing (adj)	놀라운	nol-la-un
group	무리	mu-ri
excursion, sightseeing tour	견학, 관광	gyeon-hak, gwan-gwang
guide (person)	가이드	ga-i-deu

21. Hotel

hotel	호텔	ho-tel
motel	모텔	mo-tel
three-star (~ hotel)	3성급	sam-seong-geub

five-star	5성급	o-seong-geub
to stay (in a hotel, etc.)	머무르다	meo-mu-reu-da
room	객실	gaek-sil
single room	일인실	i-rin-sil
double room	더블룸	deo-beul-lum
to book a room	방을 예약하다	bang-eul rye-yak-a-da
half board	하숙	ha-suk
full board	식사 제공	sik-sa je-gong
with bath	욕조가 있는	yok-jo-ga in-neun
with shower	샤워가 있는	sya-wo-ga in-neun
satellite television	위성 텔레비전	wi-seong tel-le-bi-jeon
air-conditioner	에어컨	e-eo-keon
towel	수건	su-geon
key	열쇠	yeol-soe
administrator	관리자	gwal-li-ja
chambermaid	객실 청소부	gaek-sil cheong-so-bu
porter	포터	po-teo
doorman	도어맨	do-eo-maen
restaurant	레스토랑	re-seu-to-rang
pub, bar	바	ba
breakfast	아침식사	a-chim-sik-sa
dinner	저녁식사	jeo-nyeok-sik-sa
buffet	뷔페	bwi-pe
lobby	로비	ro-bi
lift	엘리베이터	el-li-be-i-teo
DO NOT DISTURB	방해하지 마세요	bang-hae-ha-ji ma-se-yo
NO SMOKING	금연	geu-myeon

22. Sightseeing

monument	기념비	gi-nyeom-bi
fortress	요새	yo-sae
palace	궁전	gung-jeon
castle	성	seong
tower	탑	tap
mausoleum	영묘	yeong-myo
architecture	건축	geon-chuk
medieval (adj)	중세의	jung-se-ui
ancient (adj)	고대의	go-dae-ui
national (adj)	국가의	guk-ga-ui
famous (monument, etc.)	유명한	yu-myeong-han
tourist	관광객	gwan-gwang-gaek
guide (person)	가이드	ga-i-deu
excursion, sightseeing tour	견학, 관광	gyeon-hak, gwan-gwang
to show (vt)	보여주다	bo-yeo-ju-da

to tell (vt)	이야기하다	i-ya-gi-ha-da
to find (vt)	찾다	chat-da
to get lost (lose one's way)	길을 잃다	gi-reul ril-ta
map (e.g. underground ~)	노선도	no-seon-do
map (e.g. city ~)	지도	ji-do

souvenir, gift	기념품	gi-nyeom-pum
gift shop	기념품 가게	gi-nyeom-pum ga-ge
to take pictures	사진을 찍다	sa-ji-neul jjik-da
to have one's picture taken	사진을 찍다	sa-ji-neul jjik-da

TRANSPORT

23. Airport

airport	공항	gong-hang
aeroplane	비행기	bi-haeng-gi
airline	항공사	hang-gong-sa
air traffic controller	관제사	gwan-je-sa

departure	출발	chul-bal
arrival	도착	do-chak
to arrive (by plane)	도착하다	do-chak-a-da

| departure time | 출발시간 | chul-bal-si-gan |
| arrival time | 도착시간 | do-chak-si-gan |

| to be delayed | 연기되다 | yeon-gi-doe-da |
| flight delay | 항공기 지연 | hang-gong-gi ji-yeon |

information board	안내 전광판	an-nae jeon-gwang-pan
information	정보	jeong-bo
to announce (vt)	알리다	al-li-da
flight (e.g. next ~)	비행편	bi-haeng-pyeon

| customs | 세관 | se-gwan |
| customs officer | 세관원 | se-gwan-won |

customs declaration	세관신고서	se-gwan-sin-go-seo
to fill in the declaration	세관 신고서를 작성하다	se-gwan sin-go-seo-reul jak-seong-ha-da
passport control	여권 검사	yeo-gwon geom-sa

luggage	짐, 수하물	jim, su-ha-mul
hand luggage	휴대 가능 수하물	hyu-dae ga-neung su-ha-mul
luggage trolley	수하물 카트	su-ha-mul ka-teu

landing	착륙	chang-nyuk
landing strip	활주로	hwal-ju-ro
to land (vi)	착륙하다	chang-nyuk-a-da
airstair (passenger stair)	승강계단	seung-gang-gye-dan

check-in	체크인	che-keu-in
check-in counter	체크인 카운터	che-keu-in ka-un-teo
to check-in (vi)	체크인하다	che-keu-in-ha-da
boarding card	탑승권	tap-seung-gwon
departure gate	탑승구	tap-seung-gu

transit	트랜싯, 환승	teu-raen-sit, hwan-seung
to wait (vt)	기다리다	gi-da-ri-da
departure lounge	공항 라운지	gong-hang na-un-ji

| to see off | 배웅하다 | bae-ung-ha-da |
| to say goodbye | 작별인사를 하다 | jak-byeo-rin-sa-reul ha-da |

24. Aeroplane

aeroplane	비행기	bi-haeng-gi
air ticket	비행기표	bi-haeng-gi-pyo
airline	항공사	hang-gong-sa
airport	공항	gong-hang
supersonic (adj)	초음속의	cho-eum-so-gui

pilot	비행사	bi-haeng-sa
stewardess	승무원	seung-mu-won
navigator	항법사	hang-beop-sa

wings	날개	nal-gae
tail	꼬리	kko-ri
cockpit	조종석	jo-jong-seok
engine	엔진	en-jin
undercarriage (landing gear)	착륙 장치	chang-nyuk jang-chi
turbine	터빈	teo-bin

propeller	추진기	chu-jin-gi
black box	블랙박스	beul-laek-bak-seu
yoke (control column)	조종간	jo-jong-gan
fuel	연료	yeol-lyo

safety card	안전 안내서	an-jeon an-nae-seo
oxygen mask	산소 마스크	san-so ma-seu-keu
uniform	제복	je-bok
lifejacket	구명조끼	gu-myeong-jo-kki
parachute	낙하산	nak-a-san

takeoff	이륙	i-ryuk
to take off (vi)	이륙하다	i-ryuk-a-da
runway	활주로	hwal-ju-ro

visibility	시계	si-gye
flight (act of flying)	비행	bi-haeng
altitude	고도	go-do
air pocket	에어 포켓	e-eo po-ket

seat	자리	ja-ri
headphones	헤드폰	he-deu-pon
folding tray (tray table)	접는 테이블	jeom-neun te-i-beul
airplane window	창문	chang-mun
aisle	통로	tong-no

25. Train

| train | 기차, 열차 | gi-cha, nyeol-cha |
| commuter train | 통근 열차 | tong-geun nyeol-cha |

express train	급행 열차	geu-paeng yeol-cha
diesel locomotive	디젤 기관차	di-jel gi-gwan-cha
steam locomotive	증기 기관차	jeung-gi gi-gwan-cha

| coach, carriage | 객차 | gaek-cha |
| buffet car | 식당차 | sik-dang-cha |

rails	레일	re-il
railway	철도	cheol-do
sleeper (track support)	침목	chim-mok

platform (railway ~)	플랫폼	peul-laet-pom
platform (~ 1, 2, etc.)	길	gil
semaphore	신호기	sin-ho-gi
station	역	yeok

train driver	기관사	gi-gwan-sa
porter (of luggage)	포터	po-teo
carriage attendant	차장	cha-jang
passenger	승객	seung-gaek
ticket inspector	검표원	geom-pyo-won

| corridor (in train) | 통로 | tong-no |
| emergency brake | 비상 브레이크 | bi-sang beu-re-i-keu |

compartment	침대차	chim-dae-cha
berth	침대	chim-dae
upper berth	윗침대	wit-chim-dae
lower berth	아래 침대	a-rae chim-dae
bed linen, bedding	침구	chim-gu

ticket	표	pyo
timetable	시간표	si-gan-pyo
information display	안내 전광판	an-nae jeon-gwang-pan

to leave, to depart	떠난다	tteo-na-da
departure (of a train)	출발	chul-bal
to arrive (ab. train)	도착하다	do-chak-a-da
arrival	도착	do-chak

to arrive by train	기차로 도착하다	gi-cha-ro do-chak-a-da
to get on the train	기차에 타다	gi-cha-e ta-da
to get off the train	기차에서 내리다	gi-cha-e-seo nae-ri-da

train crash	기차 사고	gi-cha sa-go
steam locomotive	증기 기관차	jeung-gi gi-gwan-cha
stoker, fireman	화부	hwa-bu
firebox	화실	hwa-sil
coal	석탄	seok-tan

26. Ship

| ship | 배 | bae |
| vessel | 배 | bae |

steamship	증기선	jeung-gi-seon
riverboat	강배	gang-bae
cruise ship	크루즈선	keu-ru-jeu-seon
cruiser	순양함	su-nyang-ham

| yacht | 요트 | yo-teu |
| tugboat | 예인선 | ye-in-seon |

| sailing ship | 범선 | beom-seon |
| brigantine | 쌍돛대 범선 | ssang-dot-dae beom-seon |

| ice breaker | 쇄빙선 | swae-bing-seon |
| submarine | 잠수함 | jam-su-ham |

boat (flat-bottomed ~)	보트	bo-teu
dinghy (lifeboat)	종선	jong-seon
lifeboat	구조선	gu-jo-seon
motorboat	모터보트	mo-teo-bo-teu

captain	선장	seon-jang
seaman	수부	su-bu
sailor	선원	seon-won
crew	승무원	seung-mu-won

boatswain	갑판장	gap-pan-jang
cook	요리사	yo-ri-sa
ship's doctor	선의	seon-ui

deck	갑판	gap-pan
mast	돛대	dot-dae
sail	돛	dot

hold	화물칸	hwa-mul-kan
bow (prow)	이물	i-mul
stern	고물	go-mul
oar	노	no
screw propeller	스크루	seu-keu-ru

cabin	선실	seon-sil
wardroom	사관실	sa-gwan-sil
engine room	엔진실	en-jin-sil
radio room	무전실	mu-jeon-sil
wave (radio)	전파	jeon-pa

spyglass	망원경	mang-won-gyeong
bell	종	jong
flag	기	gi

| hawser (mooring ~) | 밧줄 | bat-jul |
| knot (bowline, etc.) | 매듭 | mae-deup |

| deckrails | 난간 | nan-gan |
| gangway | 사다리 | sa-da-ri |

| anchor | 닻 | dat |
| to weigh anchor | 닻을 올리다 | da-cheul rol-li-da |

| to drop anchor | 닻을 내리다 | da-cheul lae-ri-da |
| anchor chain | 닻줄 | dat-jul |

port (harbour)	항구	hang-gu
quay, wharf	부두	bu-du
to berth (moor)	정박시키다	jeong-bak-si-ki-da
to cast off	출항하다	chul-hang-ha-da

trip, voyage	여행	yeo-haeng
cruise (sea trip)	크루즈	keu-ru-jeu
course (route)	항로	hang-no
route (itinerary)	노선	no-seon

fairway (safe water channel)	항로	hang-no
shallows	얕은 곳	ya-teun got
to run aground	좌초하다	jwa-cho-ha-da

storm	폭풍우	pok-pung-u
signal	신호	sin-ho
to sink (vi)	가라앉다	ga-ra-an-da
SOS (distress signal)	조난 신호	jo-nan sin-ho
ring buoy	구명부환	gu-myeong-bu-hwan

CITY

27. Urban transport

bus, coach	버스	beo-seu
tram	전차	jeon-cha
trolleybus	트롤리 버스	teu-rol-li beo-seu
route (bus ~)	노선	no-seon
number (e.g. bus ~)	번호	beon-ho
to go by ...	... 타고 가다	... ta-go ga-da
to get on (~ the bus)	타다	ta-da
to get off ...	... 에서 내리다	... e-seo nae-ri-da
stop (e.g. bus ~)	정류장	jeong-nyu-jang
next stop	다음 정류장	da-eum jeong-nyu-jang
terminus	종점	jong-jeom
timetable	시간표	si-gan-pyo
to wait (vt)	기다리다	gi-da-ri-da
ticket	표	pyo
fare	요금	yo-geum
cashier (ticket seller)	계산원	gye-san-won
ticket inspection	검표	geom-pyo
ticket inspector	검표원	geom-pyo-won
to be late (for ...)	... 시간에 늦다	... si-gan-e neut-da
to miss (~ the train, etc.)	놓치다	no-chi-da
to be in a hurry	서두르다	seo-du-reu-da
taxi, cab	택시	taek-si
taxi driver	택시 운전 기사	taek-si un-jeon gi-sa
by taxi	택시로	taek-si-ro
taxi rank	택시 정류장	taek-si jeong-nyu-jang
to call a taxi	택시를 부르다	taek-si-reul bu-reu-da
to take a taxi	택시를 타다	taek-si-reul ta-da
traffic	교통	gyo-tong
traffic jam	교통 체증	gyo-tong che-jeung
rush hour	러시 아워	reo-si a-wo
to park (vi)	주차하다	ju-cha-ha-da
to park (vt)	주차하다	ju-cha-ha-da
car park	주차장	ju-cha-jang
underground, tube	지하철	ji-ha-cheol
station	역	yeok
to take the tube	지하철을 타다	ji-ha-cheo-reul ta-da
train	기차	gi-cha
train station	기차역	gi-cha-yeok

28. City. Life in the city

city, town	도시	do-si
capital city	수도	su-do
village	마을	ma-eul
city map	도시 지도	do-si ji-do
city centre	시내	si-nae
suburb	근교	geun-gyo
suburban (adj)	근교의	geun-gyo-ui
environs (suburbs)	주변	ju-byeon
city block	한 구획	han gu-hoek
residential block (area)	동	dong
traffic	교통	gyo-tong
traffic lights	신호등	sin-ho-deung
public transport	대중교통	dae-jung-gyo-tong
crossroads	교차로	gyo-cha-ro
zebra crossing	횡단 보도	hoeng-dan bo-do
pedestrian subway	지하 보도	ji-ha bo-do
to cross (~ the street)	건너가다	geon-neo-ga-da
pedestrian	보행자	bo-haeng-ja
pavement	인도	in-do
bridge	다리	da-ri
embankment (river walk)	강변로	gang-byeon-no
allée (garden walkway)	길	gil
park	공원	gong-won
boulevard	대로	dae-ro
square	광장	gwang-jang
avenue (wide street)	가로	ga-ro
street	거리	geo-ri
side street	골목	gol-mok
dead end	막다른길	mak-da-reun-gil
house	집	jip
building	빌딩	bil-ding
skyscraper	고층 건물	go-cheung geon-mul
facade	전면	jeon-myeon
roof	지붕	ji-bung
window	창문	chang-mun
arch	아치	a-chi
column	기둥	gi-dung
corner	모퉁이	mo-tung-i
shop window	쇼윈도우	syo-win-do-u
signboard (store sign, etc.)	간판	gan-pan
poster (e.g., playbill)	포스터	po-seu-teo
advertising poster	광고 포스터	gwang-go po-seu-teo
hoarding	광고판	gwang-go-pan
rubbish	쓰레기	sseu-re-gi

| rubbish bin | 쓰레기통 | sseu-re-gi-tong |
| rubbish dump | 쓰레기장 | sseu-re-gi-jang |

telephone box	공중 전화	gong-jung jeon-hwa
lamppost	가로등	ga-ro-deung
bench (park ~)	벤치	ben-chi

police officer	경찰관	gyeong-chal-gwan
police	경찰	gyeong-chal
beggar	거지	geo-ji
homeless (n)	노숙자	no-suk-ja

29. Urban institutions

shop	가게, 상점	ga-ge, sang-jeom
chemist, pharmacy	약국	yak-guk
optician (spectacles shop)	안경 가게	an-gyeong ga-ge
shopping centre	쇼핑몰	syo-ping-mol
supermarket	슈퍼마켓	syu-peo-ma-ket

bakery	빵집	ppang-jip
baker	제빵사	je-ppang-sa
cake shop	제과점	je-gwa-jeom
grocery shop	식료품점	sing-nyo-pum-jeom
butcher shop	정육점	jeong-yuk-jeom

| greengrocer | 야채 가게 | ya-chae ga-ge |
| market | 시장 | si-jang |

coffee bar	커피숍	keo-pi-syop
restaurant	레스토랑	re-seu-to-rang
pub, bar	바	ba
pizzeria	피자 가게	pi-ja ga-ge

hairdresser	미장원	mi-jang-won
post office	우체국	u-che-guk
dry cleaners	드라이 클리닝	deu-ra-i keul-li-ning
photo studio	사진관	sa-jin-gwan

shoe shop	신발 가게	sin-bal ga-ge
bookshop	서점	seo-jeom
sports shop	스포츠용품 매장	seu-po-cheu-yong-pum mae-jang

clothes repair shop	옷 수선 가게	ot su-seon ga-ge
formal wear hire	의류 임대	ui-ryu im-dae
video rental shop	비디오 대여	bi-di-o dae-yeo

circus	서커스	seo-keo-seu
zoo	동물원	dong-mu-rwon
cinema	영화관	yeong-hwa-gwan
museum	박물관	bang-mul-gwan
library	도서관	do-seo-gwan
theatre	극장	geuk-jang

opera (opera house)	오페라극장	o-pe-ra-geuk-jang
nightclub	나이트 클럽	na-i-teu keul-leop
casino	카지노	ka-ji-no

mosque	모스크	mo-seu-keu
synagogue	유대교 회당	yu-dae-gyo hoe-dang
cathedral	대성당	dae-seong-dang
temple	사원, 신전	sa-won, sin-jeon
church	교회	gyo-hoe

college	단과대학	dan-gwa-dae-hak
university	대학교	dae-hak-gyo
school	학교	hak-gyo

prefecture	도, 현	do, hyeon
town hall	시청	si-cheong
hotel	호텔	ho-tel
bank	은행	eun-haeng

embassy	대사관	dae-sa-gwan
travel agency	여행사	yeo-haeng-sa
information office	안내소	an-nae-so
currency exchange	환전소	hwan-jeon-so

| underground, tube | 지하철 | ji-ha-cheol |
| hospital | 병원 | byeong-won |

| petrol station | 주유소 | ju-yu-so |
| car park | 주차장 | ju-cha-jang |

30. Signs

signboard (store sign, etc.)	간판	gan-pan
notice (door sign, etc.)	안내문	an-nae-mun
poster	포스터	po-seu-teo
direction sign	방향표시	bang-hyang-pyo-si
arrow (sign)	화살표	hwa-sal-pyo

caution	경고	gyeong-go
warning sign	경고판	gyeong-go-pan
to warn (vt)	경고하다	gyeong-go-ha-da

rest day (weekly ~)	휴일	hyu-il
timetable (schedule)	시간표	si-gan-pyo
opening hours	영업 시간	yeong-eop si-gan

WELCOME!	어서 오세요!	eo-seo o-se-yo!
ENTRANCE	입구	ip-gu
WAY OUT	출구	chul-gu

PUSH	미세요	mi-se-yo
PULL	당기세요	dang-gi-se-yo
OPEN	열림	yeol-lim
CLOSED	닫힘	da-chim

| WOMEN | 여성전용 | yeo-seong-jeo-nyong |
| MEN | 남성 | nam-seong-jeo-nyong |

DISCOUNTS	할인	ha-rin
SALE	세일	se-il
NEW!	신상품	sin-sang-pum
FREE	공짜	gong-jja

ATTENTION!	주의!	ju-ui!
NO VACANCIES	빈 방 없음	bin bang eop-seum
RESERVED	예약석	ye-yak-seok

| ADMINISTRATION | 관리부 | gwal-li-bu |
| STAFF ONLY | 직원 전용 | ji-gwon jeo-nyong |

BEWARE OF THE DOG!	개조심	gae-jo-sim
NO SMOKING	금연	geu-myeon
DO NOT TOUCH!	손 대지 마시오!	son dae-ji ma-si-o!

DANGEROUS	위험	wi-heom
DANGER	위험	wi-heom
HIGH VOLTAGE	고전압	go-jeon-ap
NO SWIMMING!	수영 금지	su-yeong geum-ji
OUT OF ORDER	수리중	su-ri-jung

FLAMMABLE	가연성 물자	ga-yeon-seong mul-ja
FORBIDDEN	금지	geum-ji
NO TRESPASSING!	출입 금지	chu-rip geum-ji
WET PAINT	칠 주의	chil ju-ui

31. Shopping

to buy (purchase)	사다	sa-da
shopping	구매	gu-mae
to go shopping	쇼핑하다	syo-ping-ha-da
shopping	쇼핑	syo-ping

| to be open (ab. shop) | 열리다 | yeol-li-da |
| to be closed | 닫다 | dat-da |

footwear, shoes	신발	sin-bal
clothes, clothing	옷	ot
cosmetics	화장품	hwa-jang-pum
food products	식품	sik-pum
gift, present	선물	seon-mul

| shop assistant (masc.) | 판매원 | pan-mae-won |
| shop assistant (fem.) | 여판매원 | yeo-pan-mae-won |

cash desk	계산대	gye-san-dae
mirror	거울	geo-ul
counter (shop ~)	계산대	gye-san-dae
fitting room	탈의실	ta-rui-sil
to try on	입어보다	i-beo-bo-da

| to fit (ab. dress, etc.) | 어울리다 | eo-ul-li-da |
| to fancy (vt) | 좋아하다 | jo-a-ha-da |

price	가격	ga-gyeok
price tag	가격표	ga-gyeok-pyo
to cost (vt)	값이 … 이다	gap-si … i-da
How much?	얼마?	eol-ma?
discount	할인	ha-rin

inexpensive (adj)	비싸지 않은	bi-ssa-ji a-neun
cheap (adj)	싼	ssan
expensive (adj)	비싼	bi-ssan
It's expensive	비쌉니다	bi-ssam-ni-da

hire (n)	임대	im-dae
to hire (~ a dinner jacket)	빌리다	bil-li-da
credit (trade credit)	신용	si-nyong
on credit (adv)	신용으로	si-nyong-eu-ro

CLOTHING & ACCESSORIES

32. Outerwear. Coats

clothes	옷	ot
outerwear	겉옷	geo-tot
winter clothing	겨울옷	gyeo-u-rot

coat (overcoat)	코트	ko-teu
fur coat	모피 외투	mo-pi oe-tu
fur jacket	짧은 모피 외투	jjal-beun mo-pi oe-tu
down coat	패딩점퍼	pae-ding-jeom-peo

jacket (e.g. leather ~)	재킷	jae-kit
raincoat (trenchcoat, etc.)	트렌치코트	teu-ren-chi-ko-teu
waterproof (adj)	방수의	bang-su-ui

33. Men's & women's clothing

shirt (button shirt)	셔츠	syeo-cheu
trousers	바지	ba-ji
jeans	청바지	cheong-ba-ji
suit jacket	재킷	jae-kit
suit	양복	yang-bok

dress (frock)	드레스	deu-re-seu
skirt	치마	chi-ma
blouse	블라우스	beul-la-u-seu
knitted jacket (cardigan, etc.)	니트 재킷	ni-teu jae-kit
jacket (of a woman's suit)	재킷	jae-kit

T-shirt	티셔츠	ti-syeo-cheu
shorts (short trousers)	반바지	ban-ba-ji
tracksuit	운동복	un-dong-bok
bathrobe	목욕가운	mo-gyok-ga-un
pyjamas	파자마	pa-ja-ma

| jumper (sweater) | 스웨터 | seu-we-teo |
| pullover | 풀오버 | pu-ro-beo |

waistcoat	조끼	jo-kki
tailcoat	연미복	yeon-mi-bok
dinner suit	턱시도	teok-si-do

uniform	제복	je-bok
workwear	작업복	ja-geop-bok
boiler suit	작업바지	ja-geop-ba-ji
coat (e.g. doctor's smock)	가운	ga-un

34. Clothing. Underwear

underwear	속옷	so-got
vest (singlet)	러닝 셔츠	reo-ning syeo-cheu
socks	양말	yang-mal
nightdress	잠옷	jam-ot
bra	브라	beu-ra
knee highs (knee-high socks)	무릎길이 스타킹	mu-reup-gi-ri seu-ta-king
tights	팬티 스타킹	paen-ti seu-ta-king
stockings (hold ups)	밴드 스타킹	baen-deu seu-ta-king
swimsuit, bikini	수영복	su-yeong-bok

35. Headwear

hat	모자	mo-ja
trilby hat	중절모	jung-jeol-mo
baseball cap	야구 모자	ya-gu mo-ja
flatcap	플랫캡	peul-laet-kaep
beret	베레모	be-re-mo
hood	후드	hu-deu
panama hat	파나마 모자	pa-na-ma mo-ja
knit cap (knitted hat)	니트 모자	ni-teu mo-ja
headscarf	스카프	seu-ka-peu
women's hat	여성용 모자	yeo-seong-yong mo-ja
hard hat	안전모	an-jeon-mo
forage cap	개리슨 캡	gae-ri-seun kaep
helmet	헬멧	hel-met

36. Footwear

footwear	신발	sin-bal
shoes (men's shoes)	구두	gu-du
shoes (women's shoes)	구두	gu-du
boots (e.g., cowboy ~)	부츠	bu-cheu
carpet slippers	슬리퍼	seul-li-peo
trainers	운동화	un-dong-hwa
trainers	스니커즈	seu-ni-keo-jeu
sandals	샌들	saen-deul
cobbler (shoe repairer)	구둣방	gu-dut-bang
heel	굽	gup
pair (of shoes)	켤레	kyeol-le
lace (shoelace)	끈	kkeun
to lace up (vt)	끈을 매다	kkeu-neul mae-da
shoehorn	구둣주걱	gu-dut-ju-geok
shoe polish	구두약	gu-du-yak

37. Personal accessories

gloves	장갑	jang-gap
mittens	벙어리장갑	beong-eo-ri-jang-gap
scarf (muffler)	목도리	mok-do-ri
glasses	안경	an-gyeong
frame (eyeglass ~)	안경테	an-gyeong-te
umbrella	우산	u-san
walking stick	지팡이	ji-pang-i
hairbrush	빗, 솔빗	bit, sol-bit
fan	부채	bu-chae
tie (necktie)	넥타이	nek-ta-i
bow tie	나비넥타이	na-bi-nek-ta-i
braces	멜빵	mel-ppang
handkerchief	손수건	son-su-geon
comb	빗	bit
hair slide	머리핀	meo-ri-pin
hairpin	머리핀	meo-ri-pin
buckle	버클	beo-keul
belt	벨트	bel-teu
shoulder strap	어깨끈	eo-kkae-kkeun
bag (handbag)	가방	ga-bang
handbag	핸드백	haen-deu-baek
rucksack	배낭	bae-nang

38. Clothing. Miscellaneous

fashion	패션	pae-syeon
in vogue (adj)	유행하는	yu-haeng-ha-neun
fashion designer	패션 디자이너	pae-syeon di-ja-i-neo
collar	옷깃	ot-git
pocket	주머니, 포켓	ju-meo-ni, po-ket
pocket (as adj)	주머니의	ju-meo-ni-ui
sleeve	소매	so-mae
hanging loop	거는 끈	geo-neun kkeun
flies (on trousers)	바지 지퍼	ba-ji ji-peo
zip (fastener)	지퍼	ji-peo
fastener	조임쇠	jo-im-soe
button	단추	dan-chu
buttonhole	단춧 구멍	dan-chut gu-meong
to come off (ab. button)	떨어지다	tteo-reo-ji-da
to sew (vi, vt)	바느질하다	ba-neu-jil-ha-da
to embroider (vi, vt)	수놓다	su-no-ta
embroidery	자수	ja-su
sewing needle	바늘	ba-neul

| thread | 실 | sil |
| seam | 솔기 | sol-gi |

to get dirty (vi)	더러워지다	deo-reo-wo-ji-da
stain (mark, spot)	얼룩	eol-luk
to crease, to crumple	구겨지다	gu-gyeo-ji-da
to tear, to rip (vt)	찢다	jjit-da
clothes moth	좀	jom

39. Personal care. Cosmetics

toothpaste	치약	chi-yak
toothbrush	칫솔	chit-sol
to clean one's teeth	이를 닦다	i-reul dak-da

razor	면도기	myeon-do-gi
shaving cream	면도용 크림	myeon-do-yong keu-rim
to shave (vi)	깎다	kkak-da

| soap | 비누 | bi-nu |
| shampoo | 샴푸 | syam-pu |

scissors	가위	ga-wi
nail file	손톱줄	son-top-jul
nail clippers	손톱깎이	son-top-kka-kki
tweezers	족집게	jok-jip-ge

cosmetics	화장품	hwa-jang-pum
face mask	얼굴 마스크	eol-gul ma-seu-keu
manicure	매니큐어	mae-ni-kyu-eo
to have a manicure	매니큐어를 칠하다	mae-ni-kyu-eo-reul chil-ha-da
pedicure	페디큐어	pe-di-kyu-eo

make-up bag	화장품 가방	hwa-jang-pum ga-bang
face powder	분	bun
powder compact	콤팩트	kom-paek-teu
blusher	블러셔	beul-leo-syeo

perfume (bottled)	향수	hyang-su
toilet water (lotion)	화장수	hwa-jang-su
lotion	로션	ro-syeon
cologne	오드콜로뉴	o-deu-kol-lo-nyu

eyeshadow	아이섀도	a-i-syae-do
eyeliner	아이라이너	a-i-ra-i-neo
mascara	마스카라	ma-seu-ka-ra

lipstick	립스틱	rip-seu-tik
nail polish	매니큐어	mae-ni-kyu-eo
hair spray	헤어 스프레이	he-eo seu-peu-re-i
deodorant	데오도란트	de-o-do-ran-teu

| cream | 크림 | keu-rim |
| face cream | 얼굴 크림 | eol-gul keu-rim |

hand cream	핸드 크림	haen-deu keu-rim
anti-wrinkle cream	주름제거 크림	ju-reum-je-geo keu-rim
day (as adj)	낮의	na-jui
night (as adj)	밤의	ba-mui
tampon	탐폰	tam-pon
toilet paper (toilet roll)	화장지	hwa-jang-ji
hair dryer	헤어 드라이어	he-eo deu-ra-i-eo

40. Watches. Clocks

watch (wristwatch)	손목 시계	son-mok si-gye
dial	문자반	mun-ja-ban
hand (clock, watch)	바늘	ba-neul
metal bracelet	금속제 시계줄	geum-sok-je si-gye-jul
watch strap	시계줄	si-gye-jul
battery	건전지	geon-jeon-ji
to be flat (battery)	나가다	na-ga-da
to change a battery	배터리를 갈다	bae-teo-ri-reul gal-da
to run fast	빨리 가다	ppal-li ga-da
to run slow	늦게 가다	neut-ge ga-da
wall clock	벽시계	byeok-si-gye
hourglass	모래시계	mo-rae-si-gye
sundial	해시계	hae-si-gye
alarm clock	알람 시계	al-lam si-gye
watchmaker	시계 기술자	si-gye gi-sul-ja
to repair (vt)	수리하다	su-ri-ha-da

EVERYDAY EXPERIENCE

41. Money

money	돈	don
currency exchange	환전	hwan-jeon
exchange rate	환율	hwa-nyul
cashpoint	현금 자동 지급기	hyeon-geum ja-dong ji-geup-gi
coin	동전	dong-jeon
dollar	달러	dal-leo
euro	유로	yu-ro
lira	리라	ri-ra
Deutschmark	마르크	ma-reu-keu
franc	프랑	peu-rang
pound sterling	파운드	pa-un-deu
yen	엔	en
debt	빚	bit
debtor	채무자	chae-mu-ja
to lend (money)	빌려주다	bil-lyeo-ju-da
to borrow (vi, vt)	빌리다	bil-li-da
bank	은행	eun-haeng
account	계좌	gye-jwa
to deposit into the account	계좌에 입금하다	ip-geum-ha-da
to withdraw (vt)	출금하다	chul-geum-ha-da
credit card	신용 카드	si-nyong ka-deu
cash	현금	hyeon-geum
cheque	수표	su-pyo
to write a cheque	수표를 끊다	su-pyo-reul kkeun-ta
chequebook	수표책	su-pyo-chaek
wallet	지갑	ji-gap
purse	동전지갑	dong-jeon-ji-gap
safe	금고	geum-go
heir	상속인	sang-so-gin
inheritance	유산	yu-san
fortune (wealth)	재산, 큰돈	jae-san, keun-don
lease	임대	im-dae
rent (money)	집세	jip-se
to rent (sth from sb)	임대하다	im-dae-ha-da
price	가격	ga-gyeok
cost	비용	bi-yong

sum	액수	aek-su
to spend (vt)	쓰다	sseu-da
expenses	출비를	chul-bi-reul
to economize (vi, vt)	절약하다	jeo-ryak-a-da
economical	경제적인	gyeong-je-jeo-gin
to pay (vi, vt)	지불하다	ji-bul-ha-da
payment	지불	ji-bul
change (give the ~)	거스름돈	geo-seu-reum-don
tax	세금	se-geum
fine	벌금	beol-geum
to fine (vt)	벌금을 부과하다	beol-geu-meul bu-gwa-ha-da

42. Post. Postal service

post office	우체국	u-che-guk
post (letters, etc.)	우편물	u-pyeon-mul
postman	우체부	u-che-bu
opening hours	영업 시간	yeong-eop si-gan
letter	편지	pyeon-ji
registered letter	등기 우편	deung-gi u-pyeon
postcard	엽서	yeop-seo
telegram	전보	jeon-bo
parcel	소포	so-po
money transfer	송금	song-geum
to receive (vt)	받다	bat-da
to send (vt)	보내다	bo-nae-da
sending	발송	bal-song
address	주소	ju-so
postcode	우편 번호	u-pyeon beon-ho
sender	발송인	bal-song-in
receiver	수신인	su-sin-in
name (first name)	이름	i-reum
surname (last name)	성	seong
postage rate	요금	yo-geum
standard (adj)	일반의	il-ba-nui
economical (adj)	경제적인	gyeong-je-jeo-gin
weight	무게	mu-ge
to weigh (~ letters)	무게를 달다	mu-ge-reul dal-da
envelope	봉투	bong-tu
postage stamp	우표	u-pyo

43. Banking

| bank | 은행 | eun-haeng |
| branch (of a bank) | 지점 | ji-jeom |

| consultant | 행원 | haeng-won |
| manager (director) | 지배인 | ji-bae-in |

bank account	은행계좌	eun-haeng-gye-jwa
account number	계좌 번호	gye-jwa beon-ho
current account	당좌	dang-jwa
deposit account	보통 예금	bo-tong ye-geum

to open an account	계좌를 열다	gye-jwa-reul ryeol-da
to close the account	계좌를 해지하다	gye-jwa-reul hae-ji-ha-da
to deposit into the account	계좌에 입금하다	ip-geum-ha-da
to withdraw (vt)	출금하다	chul-geum-ha-da

deposit	저금	jeo-geum
to make a deposit	입금하다	ip-geum-ha-da
wire transfer	송금	song-geum
to wire, to transfer	송금하다	song-geum-ha-da

| sum | 액수 | aek-su |
| How much? | 얼마? | eol-ma? |

| signature | 서명 | seo-myeong |
| to sign (vt) | 서명하다 | seo-myeong-ha-da |

credit card	신용 카드	si-nyong ka-deu
code (PIN code)	비밀번호	bi-mil-beon-ho
credit card number	신용 카드 번호	si-nyong ka-deu beon-ho
cashpoint	현금 자동 지급기	hyeon-geum ja-dong ji-geup-gi

cheque	수표	su-pyo
to write a cheque	수표를 끊다	su-pyo-reul kkeun-ta
chequebook	수표책	su-pyo-chaek

loan (bank ~)	대출	dae-chul
to apply for a loan	대출 신청하다	dae-chul sin-cheong-ha-da
to get a loan	대출을 받다	dae-chu-reul bat-da
to give a loan	대출하다	dae-chul-ha-da
guarantee	담보	dam-bo

44. Telephone. Phone conversation

telephone	전화	jeon-hwa
mobile phone	휴대폰	hyu-dae-pon
answerphone	자동 응답기	ja-dong eung-dap-gi

| to call (by phone) | 전화하다 | jeon-hwa-ha-da |
| call, ring | 통화 | tong-hwa |

to dial a number	번호로 걸다	beon-ho-ro geol-da
Hello!	여보세요!	yeo-bo-se-yo!
to ask (vt)	묻다	mut-da
to answer (vi, vt)	전화를 받다	jeon-hwa-reul bat-da
to hear (vt)	듣다	deut-da

well (adv)	잘	jal
not well (adv)	좋지 않은	jo-chi a-neun
noises (interference)	잡음	ja-beum
receiver	수화기	su-hwa-gi
to pick up (~ the phone)	전화를 받다	jeon-hwa-reul bat-da
to hang up (~ the phone)	전화를 끊다	jeon-hwa-reul kkeun-ta
busy (engaged)	통화 중인	tong-hwa jung-in
to ring (ab. phone)	울리다	ul-li-da
telephone book	전화 번호부	jeon-hwa beon-ho-bu
local (adj)	시내의	si-nae-ui
trunk (e.g. ~ call)	장거리의	jang-geo-ri-ui
international (adj)	국제적인	guk-je-jeo-gin

45. Mobile telephone

mobile phone	휴대폰	hyu-dae-pon
display	화면	hwa-myeon
button	버튼	beo-teun
SIM card	SIM 카드	SIM ka-deu
battery	건전지	geon-jeon-ji
to be flat (battery)	나가다	na-ga-da
charger	충전기	chung-jeon-gi
menu	메뉴	me-nyu
settings	설정	seol-jeong
tune (melody)	벨소리	bel-so-ri
to select (vt)	선택하다	seon-taek-a-da
calculator	계산기	gye-san-gi
voice mail	자동 응답기	ja-dong eung-dap-gi
alarm clock	알람 시계	al-lam si-gye
contacts	연락처	yeol-lak-cheo
SMS (text message)	문자 메시지	mun-ja me-si-ji
subscriber	가입자	ga-ip-ja

46. Stationery

ballpoint pen	볼펜	bol-pen
fountain pen	만년필	man-nyeon-pil
pencil	연필	yeon-pil
highlighter	형광펜	hyeong-gwang-pen
felt-tip pen	사인펜	sa-in-pen
notepad	공책	gong-chaek
diary	수첩	su-cheop
ruler	자	ja

calculator	계산기	gye-san-gi
rubber	지우개	ji-u-gae
drawing pin	압정	ap-jeong
paper clip	클립	keul-lip
glue	접착제	jeop-chak-je
stapler	호치키스	ho-chi-ki-seu
hole punch	펀치	peon-chi
pencil sharpener	연필깎이	yeon-pil-kka-kki

47. Foreign languages

language	언어	eon-eo
foreign language	외국어	oe-gu-geo
to study (vt)	공부하다	gong-bu-ha-da
to learn (language, etc.)	배우다	bae-u-da
to read (vi, vt)	읽다	ik-da
to speak (vi, vt)	말하다	mal-ha-da
to understand (vt)	이해하다	i-hae-ha-da
to write (vt)	쓰다	sseu-da
fast (adv)	빨리	ppal-li
slowly (adv)	천천히	cheon-cheon-hi
fluently (adv)	유창하게	yu-chang-ha-ge
rules	규칙	gyu-chik
grammar	문법	mun-beop
vocabulary	어휘	eo-hwi
phonetics	음성학	eum-seong-hak
textbook	교과서	gyo-gwa-seo
dictionary	사전	sa-jeon
teach-yourself book	자습서	ja-seup-seo
phrasebook	회화집	hoe-hwa-jip
cassette, tape	테이프	te-i-peu
videotape	비디오테이프	bi-di-o-te-i-peu
CD, compact disc	씨디	ssi-di
DVD	디비디	di-bi-di
alphabet	알파벳	al-pa-bet
to spell (vt)	… 의 철자이다	… ui cheol-ja-i-da
pronunciation	발음	ba-reum
accent	악센트	ak-sen-teu
with an accent	사투리로	sa-tu-ri-ro
without an accent	억양 없이	eo-gyang eop-si
word	단어	dan-eo
meaning	의미	ui-mi
course (e.g. a French ~)	강좌	gang-jwa
to sign up	등록하다	deung-nok-a-da

teacher	강사	gang-sa
translation (process)	번역	beo-nyeok
translation (text, etc.)	번역	beo-nyeok
translator	번역가	beo-nyeok-ga
interpreter	통역가	tong-yeok-ga
polyglot	수개 국어를 말하는 사람	su-gae gu-geo-reul mal-ha-neun sa-ram
memory	기억력	gi-eong-nyeok

MEALS. RESTAURANT

48. Table setting

spoon	숟가락	sut-ga-rak
knife	나이프	na-i-peu
fork	포크	po-keu
cup (e.g., coffee ~)	컵	keop
plate (dinner ~)	접시	jeop-si
saucer	받침 접시	bat-chim jeop-si
serviette	냅킨	naep-kin
toothpick	이쑤시개	i-ssu-si-gae

49. Restaurant

restaurant	레스토랑	re-seu-to-rang
coffee bar	커피숍	keo-pi-syop
pub, bar	바	ba
tearoom	카페, 티룸	ka-pe, ti-rum
waiter	웨이터	we-i-teo
waitress	웨이트리스	we-i-teu-ri-seu
barman	바텐더	ba-ten-deo
menu	메뉴판	me-nyu-pan
wine list	와인 메뉴	wa-in me-nyu
to book a table	테이블 예약을 하다	te-i-beul rye-ya-geul ha-da
course, dish	요리, 코스	yo-ri, ko-seu
to order (meal)	주문하다	ju-mun-ha-da
to make an order	주문을 하다	ju-mu-neul ha-da
aperitif	아페리티프	a-pe-ri-ti-peu
starter	애피타이저	ae-pi-ta-i-jeo
dessert, pudding	디저트	di-jeo-teu
bill	계산서	gye-san-seo
to pay the bill	계산하다	gye-san-ha-da
to give change	거스름돈을 주다	geo-seu-reum-do-neul ju-da
tip	팁	tip

50. Meals

food	음식	eum-sik
to eat (vi, vt)	먹다	meok-da

breakfast	아침식사	a-chim-sik-sa
to have breakfast	아침을 먹다	a-chi-meul meok-da
lunch	점심식사	jeom-sim-sik-sa
to have lunch	점심을 먹다	jeom-si-meul meok-da
dinner	저녁식사	jeo-nyeok-sik-sa
to have dinner	저녁을 먹다	jeo-nyeo-geul meok-da
appetite	식욕	si-gyok
Enjoy your meal!	맛있게 드십시오!	man-nit-ge deu-sip-si-o!
to open (~ a bottle)	열다	yeol-da
to spill (liquid)	엎지르다	eop-ji-reu-da
to spill out (vi)	쏟아지다	sso-da-ji-da
to boil (vi)	끓다	kkeul-ta
to boil (vt)	끓이다	kkeu-ri-da
boiled (~ water)	끓인	kkeu-rin
to chill, cool down (vt)	식히다	sik-i-da
to chill (vi)	식다	sik-da
taste, flavour	맛	mat
aftertaste	뒷 맛	dwit mat
to slim down (lose weight)	살을 빼다	sa-reul ppae-da
diet	다이어트	da-i-eo-teu
vitamin	비타민	bi-ta-min
calorie	칼로리	kal-lo-ri
vegetarian (n)	채식주의자	chae-sik-ju-ui-ja
vegetarian (adj)	채식주의의	chae-sik-ju-ui-ui
fats (nutrient)	지방	ji-bang
proteins	단백질	dan-baek-jil
carbohydrates	탄수화물	tan-su-hwa-mul
slice (of lemon, ham)	조각	jo-gak
piece (of cake, pie)	조각	jo-gak
crumb (of bread, cake, etc.)	부스러기	bu-seu-reo-gi

51. Cooked dishes

course, dish	요리, 코스	yo-ri, ko-seu
cuisine	요리	yo-ri
recipe	요리법	yo-ri-beop
portion	분량	bul-lyang
salad	샐러드	sael-leo-deu
soup	수프	su-peu
clear soup (broth)	육수	yuk-su
sandwich (bread)	샌드위치	saen-deu-wi-chi
fried eggs	계란후라이	gye-ran-hu-ra-i
hamburger (beefburger)	햄버거	haem-beo-geo
beefsteak	비프스테이크	bi-peu-seu-te-i-keu

side dish	사이드 메뉴	sa-i-deu me-nyu
spaghetti	스파게티	seu-pa-ge-ti
mash	으깬 감자	eu-kkaen gam-ja
pizza	피자	pi-ja
porridge (oatmeal, etc.)	죽	juk
omelette	오믈렛	o-meul-let

boiled (e.g. ~ beef)	삶은	sal-meun
smoked (adj)	훈제된	hun-je-doen
fried (adj)	튀긴	twi-gin
dried (adj)	말린	mal-lin
frozen (adj)	얼린	eol-lin
pickled (adj)	초절인	cho-jeo-rin

sweet (sugary)	단	dan
salty (adj)	짠	jjan
cold (adj)	차가운	cha-ga-un
hot (adj)	뜨거운	tteu-geo-un
bitter (adj)	쓴	sseun
tasty (adj)	맛있는	man-nin-neun

to cook in boiling water	삶다	sam-da
to cook (dinner)	요리하다	yo-ri-ha-da
to fry (vt)	부치다	bu-chi-da
to heat up (food)	데우다	de-u-da

to salt (vt)	소금을 넣다	so-geu-meul leo-ta
to pepper (vt)	후추를 넣다	hu-chu-reul leo-ta
to grate (vt)	강판에 갈다	gang-pa-ne gal-da
peel (n)	껍질	kkeop-jil
to peel (vt)	껍질 벗기다	kkeop-jil beot-gi-da

52. Food

meat	고기	go-gi
chicken	닭고기	dak-go-gi
poussin	영계	yeong-gye
duck	오리고기	o-ri-go-gi
goose	거위고기	geo-wi-go-gi
game	사냥감	sa-nyang-gam
turkey	칠면조고기	chil-myeon-jo-go-gi

pork	돼지고기	dwae-ji-go-gi
veal	송아지 고기	song-a-ji go-gi
lamb	양고기	yang-go-gi
beef	소고기	so-go-gi
rabbit	토끼고기	to-kki-go-gi

sausage (bologna, etc.)	소시지	so-si-ji
vienna sausage (frankfurter)	비엔나 소시지	bi-en-na so-si-ji
bacon	베이컨	be-i-keon
ham	햄	haem
gammon	개먼	gae-meon
pâté	파테	pa-te

liver	간	gan
mince (minced meat)	다진 고기	da-jin go-gi
tongue	혀	hyeo
egg	계란	gye-ran
eggs	계란	gye-ran
egg white	흰자	huin-ja
egg yolk	노른자	no-reun-ja
fish	생선	saeng-seon
seafood	해물	hae-mul
caviar	캐비어	kae-bi-eo
crab	게	ge
prawn	새우	sae-u
oyster	굴	gul
spiny lobster	대하	dae-ha
octopus	문어	mun-eo
squid	오징어	o-jing-eo
sturgeon	철갑상어	cheol-gap-sang-eo
salmon	연어	yeon-eo
halibut	넙치	neop-chi
cod	대구	dae-gu
mackerel	고등어	go-deung-eo
tuna	참치	cham-chi
eel	뱀장어	baem-jang-eo
trout	송어	song-eo
sardine	정어리	jeong-eo-ri
pike	강꼬치고기	gang-kko-chi-go-gi
herring	청어	cheong-eo
bread	빵	ppang
cheese	치즈	chi-jeu
sugar	설탕	seol-tang
salt	소금	so-geum
rice	쌀	ssal
pasta (macaroni)	파스타	pa-seu-ta
noodles	면	myeon
butter	버터	beo-teo
vegetable oil	식물유	sing-mu-ryu
sunflower oil	해바라기유	hae-ba-ra-gi-yu
margarine	마가린	ma-ga-rin
olives	올리브	ol-li-beu
olive oil	올리브유	ol-li-beu-yu
milk	우유	u-yu
condensed milk	연유	yeo-nyu
yogurt	요구르트	yo-gu-reu-teu
soured cream	사워크림	sa-wo-keu-rim
cream (of milk)	크림	keu-rim

| mayonnaise | 마요네즈 | ma-yo-ne-jeu |
| buttercream | 버터크림 | beo-teo-keu-rim |

groats (barley ~, etc.)	곡물	gong-mul
flour	밀가루	mil-ga-ru
tinned food	통조림	tong-jo-rim

cornflakes	콘플레이크	kon-peul-le-i-keu
honey	꿀	kkul
jam	잼	jaem
chewing gum	껌	kkeom

53. Drinks

water	물	mul
drinking water	음료수	eum-nyo-su
mineral water	미네랄 워터	mi-ne-ral rwo-teo

still (adj)	탄산 없는	tan-san neom-neun
carbonated (adj)	탄산의	tan-sa-nui
sparkling (adj)	탄산이 든	tan-san-i deun
ice	얼음	eo-reum
with ice	얼음을 넣은	eo-reu-meul leo-eun

non-alcoholic (adj)	무알코올의	mu-al-ko-o-rui
soft drink	청량음료	cheong-nyang-eum-nyo
refreshing drink	청량 음료	cheong-nyang eum-nyo
lemonade	레모네이드	re-mo-ne-i-deu

spirits	술	sul
wine	와인	wa-in
white wine	백 포도주	baek po-do-ju
red wine	레드 와인	re-deu wa-in

liqueur	리큐르	ri-kyu-reu
champagne	샴페인	syam-pe-in
vermouth	베르무트	be-reu-mu-teu

whisky	위스키	wi-seu-ki
vodka	보드카	bo-deu-ka
gin	진	jin
cognac	코냑	ko-nyak
rum	럼	reom

coffee	커피	keo-pi
black coffee	블랙 커피	beul-laek keo-pi
white coffee	밀크 커피	mil-keu keo-pi
cappuccino	카푸치노	ka-pu-chi-no
instant coffee	인스턴트 커피	in-seu-teon-teu keo-pi

milk	우유	u-yu
cocktail	칵테일	kak-te-il
milkshake	밀크 셰이크	mil-keu sye-i-keu
juice	주스	ju-seu

tomato juice	토마토 주스	to-ma-to ju-seu
orange juice	오렌지 주스	o-ren-ji ju-seu
freshly squeezed juice	생과일주스	saeng-gwa-il-ju-seu
beer	맥주	maek-ju
lager	라거	ra-geo
bitter	흑맥주	heung-maek-ju
tea	차	cha
black tea	홍차	hong-cha
green tea	녹차	nok-cha

54. Vegetables

vegetables	채소	chae-so
greens	녹황색 채소	nok-wang-saek chae-so
tomato	토마토	to-ma-to
cucumber	오이	o-i
carrot	당근	dang-geun
potato	감자	gam-ja
onion	양파	yang-pa
garlic	마늘	ma-neul
cabbage	양배추	yang-bae-chu
cauliflower	컬리플라워	keol-li-peul-la-wo
Brussels sprouts	방울다다기 양배추	bang-ul-da-da-gi yang-bae-chu
broccoli	브로콜리	beu-ro-kol-li
beetroot	비트	bi-teu
aubergine	가지	ga-ji
courgette	애호박	ae-ho-bak
pumpkin	호박	ho-bak
turnip	순무	sun-mu
parsley	파슬리	pa-seul-li
dill	딜	dil
lettuce	양상추	yang-sang-chu
celery	셀러리	sel-leo-ri
asparagus	아스파라거스	a-seu-pa-ra-geo-seu
spinach	시금치	si-geum-chi
pea	완두	wan-du
beans	콩	kong
maize	옥수수	ok-su-su
kidney bean	강낭콩	gang-nang-kong
sweet paper	피망	pi-mang
radish	무	mu
artichoke	아티초크	a-ti-cho-keu

55. Fruits. Nuts

fruit	과일	gwa-il
apple	사과	sa-gwa
pear	배	bae
lemon	레몬	re-mon
orange	오렌지	o-ren-ji
strawberry (garden ~)	딸기	ttal-gi
tangerine	귤	gyul
plum	자두	ja-du
peach	복숭아	bok-sung-a
apricot	살구	sal-gu
raspberry	라즈베리	ra-jeu-be-ri
pineapple	파인애플	pa-in-ae-peul
banana	바나나	ba-na-na
watermelon	수박	su-bak
grape	포도	po-do
sour cherry	신양	si-nyang
sweet cherry	양벚나무	yang-beon-na-mu
melon	멜론	mel-lon
grapefruit	자몽	ja-mong
avocado	아보카도	a-bo-ka-do
papaya	파파야	pa-pa-ya
mango	망고	mang-go
pomegranate	석류	seong-nyu
redcurrant	레드커렌트	re-deu-keo-ren-teu
blackcurrant	블랙커렌트	beul-laek-keo-ren-teu
gooseberry	구스베리	gu-seu-be-ri
bilberry	빌베리	bil-be-ri
blackberry	블랙베리	beul-laek-be-ri
raisin	건포도	geon-po-do
fig	무화과	mu-hwa-gwa
date	대추야자	dae-chu-ya-ja
peanut	땅콩	ttang-kong
almond	아몬드	a-mon-deu
walnut	호두	ho-du
hazelnut	개암	gae-am
coconut	코코넛	ko-ko-neot
pistachios	피스타치오	pi-seu-ta-chi-o

56. Bread. Sweets

bakers' confectionery (pastry)	과자류	gwa-ja-ryu
bread	빵	ppang
biscuits	쿠키	ku-ki
chocolate (n)	초콜릿	cho-kol-lit
chocolate (as adj)	초콜릿의	cho-kol-lis-ui

candy (wrapped)	사탕	sa-tang
cake (e.g. cupcake)	케이크	ke-i-keu
cake (e.g. birthday ~)	케이크	ke-i-keu
pie (e.g. apple ~)	파이	pa-i
filling (for cake, pie)	속	sok
jam (whole fruit jam)	잼	jaem
marmalade	마멀레이드	ma-meol-le-i-deu
wafers	와플	wa-peul
ice-cream	아이스크림	a-i-seu-keu-rim

57. Spices

salt	소금	so-geum
salty (adj)	짜	jja
to salt (vt)	소금을 넣다	so-geu-meul leo-ta
black pepper	후추	hu-chu
red pepper (milled ~)	고춧가루	go-chut-ga-ru
mustard	겨자	gyeo-ja
horseradish	고추냉이	go-chu-naeng-i
condiment	양념	yang-nyeom
spice	향료	hyang-nyo
sauce	소스	so-seu
vinegar	식초	sik-cho
anise	아니스	a-ni-seu
basil	바질	ba-jil
cloves	정향	jeong-hyang
ginger	생강	saeng-gang
coriander	고수	go-su
cinnamon	계피	gye-pi
sesame	깨	kkae
bay leaf	월계수잎	wol-gye-su-ip
paprika	파프리카	pa-peu-ri-ka
caraway	캐러웨이	kae-reo-we-i
saffron	사프란	sa-peu-ran

PERSONAL INFORMATION. FAMILY

58. Personal information. Forms

name (first name)	이름	i-reum
surname (last name)	성	seong
date of birth	생년월일	saeng-nyeon-wo-ril
place of birth	탄생지	tan-saeng-ji
nationality	국적	guk-jeok
place of residence	거소	geo-so
country	나라	na-ra
profession (occupation)	직업	ji-geop
gender, sex	성별	seong-byeol
height	키	ki
weight	몸무게	mom-mu-ge

59. Family members. Relatives

mother	어머니	eo-meo-ni
father	아버지	a-beo-ji
son	아들	a-deul
daughter	딸	ttal
younger daughter	작은딸	ja-geun-ttal
younger son	작은아들	ja-geun-a-deul
eldest daughter	맏딸	mat-ttal
eldest son	맏아들	ma-da-deul
brother	형제	hyeong-je
sister	자매	ja-mae
cousin (masc.)	사촌 형제	sa-chon hyeong-je
cousin (fem.)	사촌 자매	sa-chon ja-mae
mummy	엄마	eom-ma
dad, daddy	아빠	a-ppa
parents	부모	bu-mo
child	아이, 아동	a-i, a-dong
children	아이들	a-i-deul
grandmother	할머니	hal-meo-ni
grandfather	할아버지	ha-ra-beo-ji
grandson	손자	son-ja
granddaughter	손녀	son-nyeo
grandchildren	손자들	son-ja-deul
uncle	삼촌	sam-chon

nephew	조카	jo-ka
niece	조카딸	jo-ka-ttal
mother-in-law (wife's mother)	장모	jang-mo
father-in-law (husband's father)	시아버지	si-a-beo-ji
son-in-law (daughter's husband)	사위	sa-wi
stepmother	계모	gye-mo
stepfather	계부	gye-bu
infant	영아	yeong-a
baby (infant)	아기	a-gi
little boy, kid	꼬마	kko-ma
wife	아내	a-nae
husband	남편	nam-pyeon
spouse (husband)	배우자	bae-u-ja
spouse (wife)	배우자	bae-u-ja
married (masc.)	결혼한	gyeol-hon-han
married (fem.)	결혼한	gyeol-hon-han
single (unmarried)	미혼의	mi-hon-ui
bachelor	미혼 남자	mi-hon nam-ja
divorced (masc.)	이혼한	i-hon-han
widow	과부	gwa-bu
widower	홀아비	ho-ra-bi
relative	친척	chin-cheok
close relative	가까운 친척	ga-kka-un chin-cheok
distant relative	먼 친척	meon chin-cheok
relatives	친척들	chin-cheok-deul
orphan (boy or girl)	고아	go-a
guardian (of a minor)	후견인	hu-gyeon-in
to adopt (a boy)	입양하다	i-byang-ha-da
to adopt (a girl)	입양하다	i-byang-ha-da

60. Friends. Colleagues

friend (masc.)	친구	chin-gu
friend (fem.)	친구	chin-gu
friendship	우정	u-jeong
to be friends	사귀다	sa-gwi-da
pal (masc.)	벗	beot
pal (fem.)	벗	beot
partner	파트너	pa-teu-neo
chief (boss)	상사	sang-sa
superior (n)	윗사람	wit-sa-ram
subordinate (n)	부하	bu-ha
colleague	동료	dong-nyo

acquaintance (person)	아는 사람	a-neun sa-ram
fellow traveller	동행자	dong-haeng-ja
classmate	동급생	dong-geup-saeng
neighbour (masc.)	이웃	i-ut
neighbour (fem.)	이웃	i-ut
neighbours	이웃들	i-ut-deul

HUMAN BODY. MEDICINE

61. Head

head	머리	meo-ri
face	얼굴	eol-gul
nose	코	ko
mouth	입	ip
eye	눈	nun
eyes	눈	nun
pupil	눈동자	nun-dong-ja
eyebrow	눈썹	nun-sseop
eyelash	속눈썹	song-nun-sseop
eyelid	눈꺼풀	nun-kkeo-pul
tongue	혀	hyeo
tooth	이	i
lips	입술	ip-sul
cheekbones	광대뼈	gwang-dae-ppyeo
gum	잇몸	in-mom
palate	입천장	ip-cheon-jang
nostrils	콧구멍	kot-gu-meong
chin	턱	teok
jaw	턱	teok
cheek	뺨, 볼	ppyam, bol
forehead	이마	i-ma
temple	관자놀이	gwan-ja-no-ri
ear	귀	gwi
back of the head	뒤통수	dwi-tong-su
neck	목	mok
throat	목구멍	mok-gu-meong
hair	머리털, 헤어	meo-ri-teol, he-eo
hairstyle	머리 스타일	meo-ri seu-ta-il
haircut	헤어컷	he-eo-keot
wig	가발	ga-bal
moustache	콧수염	kot-su-yeom
beard	턱수염	teok-su-yeom
to have (a beard, etc.)	기르다	gi-reu-da
plait	땋은 머리	tta-eun meo-ri
sideboards	구레나룻	gu-re-na-rut
red-haired (adj)	빨강머리의	ppal-gang-meo-ri-ui
grey (hair)	흰머리의	huin-meo-ri-ui
bald (adj)	대머리인	dae-meo-ri-in
bald patch	땜통	ttaem-tong

| ponytail | 말총머리 | mal-chong-meo-ri |
| fringe | 앞머리 | am-meo-ri |

62. Human body

| hand | 손 | son |
| arm | 팔 | pal |

finger	손가락	son-ga-rak
thumb	엄지손가락	eom-ji-son-ga-rak
little finger	새끼손가락	sae-kki-son-ga-rak
nail	손톱	son-top

fist	주먹	ju-meok
palm	손바닥	son-ba-dak
wrist	손목	son-mok
forearm	전박	jeon-bak
elbow	팔꿈치	pal-kkum-chi
shoulder	어깨	eo-kkae

leg	다리	da-ri
foot	발	bal
knee	무릎	mu-reup
calf	종아리	jong-a-ri
hip	엉덩이	eong-deong-i
heel	발뒤꿈치	bal-dwi-kkum-chi

body	몸	mom
stomach	배	bae
chest	가슴	ga-seum
breast	가슴	ga-seum
flank	옆구리	yeop-gu-ri
back	등	deung
lower back	허리	heo-ri
waist	허리	heo-ri

navel (belly button)	배꼽	bae-kkop
buttocks	엉덩이	eong-deong-i
bottom	엉덩이	eong-deong-i

beauty spot	점	jeom
birthmark (café au lait spot)	모반	mo-ban
tattoo	문신	mun-sin
scar	흉터	hyung-teo

63. Diseases

illness	병	byeong
to be ill	눕다	nup-da
health	건강	geon-gang
runny nose (coryza)	비염	bi-yeom
tonsillitis	편도염	pyeon-do-yeom

| cold (illness) | 감기 | gam-gi |
| to catch a cold | 감기에 걸리다 | gam-gi-e geol-li-da |

bronchitis	기관지염	gi-gwan-ji-yeom
pneumonia	폐렴	pye-ryeom
flu, influenza	독감	dok-gam

shortsighted (adj)	근시의	geun-si-ui
longsighted (adj)	원시의	won-si-ui
strabismus (crossed eyes)	사시	sa-si
squint-eyed (adj)	사시인	sa-si-in
cataract	백내장	baeng-nae-jang
glaucoma	녹내장	nong-nae-jang

stroke	뇌졸중	noe-jol-jung
heart attack	심장마비	sim-jang-ma-bi
myocardial infarction	심근경색증	sim-geun-gyeong-saek-jeung
paralysis	마비	ma-bi
to paralyse (vt)	마비되다	ma-bi-doe-da

allergy	알레르기	al-le-reu-gi
asthma	천식	cheon-sik
diabetes	당뇨병	dang-nyo-byeong

| toothache | 치통, 이앓이 | chi-tong, i-a-ri |
| caries | 충치 | chung-chi |

diarrhoea	설사	seol-sa
constipation	변비증	byeon-bi-jeung
stomach upset	배탈	bae-tal
food poisoning	식중독	sik-jung-dok
to get food poisoning	식중독에 걸리다	sik-jung-do-ge geol-li-da

arthritis	관절염	gwan-jeo-ryeom
rickets	구루병	gu-ru-byeong
rheumatism	류머티즘	ryu-meo-ti-jeum

gastritis	위염	wi-yeom
appendicitis	맹장염	maeng-jang-yeom
cholecystitis	담낭염	dam-nang-yeom
ulcer	궤양	gwe-yang

measles	홍역	hong-yeok
rubella (German measles)	풍진	pung-jin
jaundice	황달	hwang-dal
hepatitis	간염	gan-nyeom

schizophrenia	정신 분열증	jeong-sin bu-nyeol-jeung
rabies (hydrophobia)	광견병	gwang-gyeon-byeong
neurosis	신경증	sin-gyeong-jeung
concussion	뇌진탕	noe-jin-tang

cancer	암	am
sclerosis	경화증	gyeong-hwa-jeung
multiple sclerosis	다발성 경화증	da-bal-seong gyeong-hwa-jeung

alcoholism	알코올 중독	al-ko-ol jung-dok
alcoholic (n)	알코올 중독자	al-ko-ol jung-dok-ja
syphilis	매독	mae-dok
AIDS	에이즈	e-i-jeu

tumour	종양	jong-yang
malignant (adj)	악성의	ak-seong-ui
benign (adj)	양성의	yang-seong-ui

fever	열병	yeol-byeong
malaria	말라리아	mal-la-ri-a
gangrene	괴저	goe-jeo
seasickness	뱃멀미	baen-meol-mi
epilepsy	간질	gan-jil

epidemic	유행병	yu-haeng-byeong
typhus	발진티푸스	bal-jin-ti-pu-seu
tuberculosis	결핵	gyeol-haek
cholera	콜레라	kol-le-ra
plague (bubonic ~)	페스트	pe-seu-teu

64. Symptoms. Treatments. Part 1

symptom	증상	jeung-sang
temperature	체온	che-on
high temperature (fever)	열	yeol
pulse (heartbeat)	맥박	maek-bak

dizziness (vertigo)	현기증	hyeon-gi-jeung
hot (adj)	뜨거운	tteu-geo-un
shivering	전율	jeo-nyul
pale (e.g. ~ face)	창백한	chang-baek-an

cough	기침	gi-chim
to cough (vi)	기침을 하다	gi-chi-meul ha-da
to sneeze (vi)	재채기하다	jae-chae-gi-ha-da
faint	실신	sil-sin
to faint (vi)	실신하다	sil-sin-ha-da

bruise (hématome)	멍	meong
bump (lump)	혹	hok
to bang (bump)	부딪치다	bu-dit-chi-da
contusion (bruise)	타박상	ta-bak-sang
to get a bruise	타박상을 입다	ta-bak-sang-eul rip-da

to limp (vi)	절다	jeol-da
dislocation	탈구	tal-gu
to dislocate (vt)	탈구하다	tal-gu-ha-da
fracture	골절	gol-jeol
to have a fracture	골절하다	gol-jeol-ha-da

cut (e.g. paper ~)	베인	be-in
to cut oneself	베다	jeol-chang-eul rip-da
bleeding	출혈	chul-hyeol

burn (injury)	화상	hwa-sang
to get burned	데다	de-da
to prick (vt)	찌르다	jji-reu-da
to prick oneself	찔리다	jjil-li-da
to injure (vt)	다치다	da-chi-da
injury	부상	bu-sang
wound	부상	bu-sang
trauma	정신적 외상	jeong-sin-jeok goe-sang
to be delirious	망상을 겨다	mang-sang-eul gyeok-da
to stutter (vi)	말을 더듬다	ma-reul deo-deum-da
sunstroke	일사병	il-sa-byeong

65. Symptoms. Treatments. Part 2

pain, ache	통증	tong-jeung
splinter (in foot, etc.)	가시	ga-si
sweat (perspiration)	땀	ttam
to sweat (perspire)	땀이 나다	ttam-i na-da
vomiting	구토	gu-to
convulsions	경련	gyeong-nyeon
pregnant (adj)	임신한	im-sin-han
to be born	태어나다	tae-eo-na-da
delivery, labour	출산	chul-san
to deliver (~ a baby)	낳다	na-ta
abortion	낙태	nak-tae
breathing, respiration	호흡	ho-heup
in-breath (inhalation)	들숨	deul-sum
out-breath (exhalation)	날숨	nal-sum
to exhale (breathe out)	내쉬다	nae-swi-da
to inhale (vi)	들이쉬다	deu-ri-swi-da
disabled person	장애인	jang-ae-in
cripple	병신	byeong-sin
drug addict	마약 중독자	ma-yak jung-dok-ja
deaf (adj)	귀가 먼	gwi-ga meon
mute (adj)	벙어리인	beong-eo-ri-in
deaf mute (adj)	농아인	nong-a-in
mad, insane (adj)	미친	mi-chin
madman (demented person)	광인	gwang-in
madwoman	광인	gwang-in
to go insane	미치다	mi-chi-da
gene	유전자	yu-jeon-ja
immunity	면역성	myeo-nyeok-seong
hereditary (adj)	유전의	yu-jeon-ui
congenital (adj)	선천적인	seon-cheon-jeo-gin

virus	바이러스	ba-i-reo-seu
microbe	미생물	mi-saeng-mul
bacterium	세균	se-gyun
infection	감염	gam-nyeom

66. Symptoms. Treatments. Part 3

| hospital | 병원 | byeong-won |
| patient | 환자 | hwan-ja |

diagnosis	진단	jin-dan
cure	치료	chi-ryo
to get treatment	치료를 받다	chi-ryo-reul bat-da
to treat (~ a patient)	치료하다	chi-ryo-ha-da
to nurse (look after)	간호하다	gan-ho-ha-da
care (nursing ~)	간호	gan-ho

operation, surgery	수술	su-sul
to bandage (head, limb)	붕대를 감다	bung-dae-reul gam-da
bandaging	붕대	bung-dae

vaccination	예방주사	ye-bang-ju-sa
to vaccinate (vt)	접종하다	jeop-jong-ha-da
injection	주사	ju-sa
to give an injection	주사하다	ju-sa-ha-da

amputation	절단	jeol-dan
to amputate (vt)	절단하다	jeol-dan-ha-da
coma	혼수 상태	hon-su sang-tae
to be in a coma	혼수 상태에 있다	hon-su sang-tae-e it-da
intensive care	집중 치료	jip-jung chi-ryo

to recover (~ from flu)	회복하다	hoe-bok-a-da
condition (patient's ~)	상태	sang-tae
consciousness	의식	ui-sik
memory (faculty)	기억	gi-eok

to pull out (tooth)	빼다	ppae-da
filling	충전물	chung-jeon-mul
to fill (a tooth)	때우다	ttae-u-da

| hypnosis | 최면 | choe-myeon |
| to hypnotize (vt) | 최면을 걸다 | choe-myeo-neul geol-da |

67. Medicine. Drugs. Accessories

medicine, drug	약	yak
remedy	약제	yak-je
prescription	처방	cheo-bang

| tablet, pill | 정제 | jeong-je |
| ointment | 연고 | yeon-go |

ampoule	앰풀	aem-pul
mixture, solution	혼합물	hon-ham-mul
syrup	물약	mul-lyak
capsule	알약	a-ryak
powder	가루약	ga-ru-yak
gauze bandage	거즈 붕대	geo-jeu bung-dae
cotton wool	솜	som
iodine	요오드	yo-o-deu
plaster	반창고	ban-chang-go
eyedropper	점안기	jeom-an-gi
thermometer	체온계	che-on-gye
syringe	주사기	ju-sa-gi
wheelchair	휠체어	hwil-che-eo
crutches	목발	mok-bal
painkiller	진통제	jin-tong-je
laxative	완하제	wan-ha-je
spirits (ethanol)	알코올	al-ko-ol
medicinal herbs	약초	yak-cho
herbal (~ tea)	약초의	yak-cho-ui

FLAT

flat	아파트	a-pa-teu
room	방	bang
bedroom	침실	chim-sil
dining room	식당	sik-dang
living room	거실	geo-sil
study (home office)	서재	seo-jae
entry room	곁방	gyeot-bang
bathroom	욕실	yok-sil
water closet	화장실	hwa-jang-sil
ceiling	천장	cheon-jang
floor	마루	ma-ru
corner	구석	gu-seok

69. Furniture. Interior

furniture	가구	ga-gu
table	식탁, 테이블	sik-tak, te-i-beul
chair	의자	ui-ja
bed	침대	chim-dae
sofa, settee	소파	so-pa
armchair	안락 의자	al-lak gui-ja
bookcase	책장	chaek-jang
shelf	책꽂이	chaek-kko-ji
wardrobe	옷장	ot-jang
coat rack (wall-mounted ~)	옷걸이	ot-geo-ri
coat stand	스탠드옷걸이	seu-taen-deu-ot-geo-ri
chest of drawers	서랍장	seo-rap-jang
coffee table	커피 테이블	keo-pi te-i-beul
mirror	거울	geo-ul
carpet	양탄자	yang-tan-ja
small carpet	러그	reo-geu
fireplace	벽난로	byeong-nan-no
candle	초	cho
candlestick	촛대	chot-dae
drapes	커튼	keo-teun
wallpaper	벽지	byeok-ji

blinds (jalousie)	블라인드	beul-la-in-deu
table lamp	테이블 램프	deung
wall lamp (sconce)	벽등	byeok-deung
standard lamp	플로어 스탠드	peul-lo-eo seu-taen-deu
chandelier	샹들리에	syang-deul-li-e
leg (of a chair, table)	다리	da-ri
armrest	팔걸이	pal-geo-ri
back (backrest)	등받이	deung-ba-ji
drawer	서랍	seo-rap

70. Bedding

bedclothes	침구	chim-gu
pillow	베개	be-gae
pillowslip	베갯잇	be-gaen-nit
duvet	이불	i-bul
sheet	시트	si-teu
bedspread	침대보	chim-dae-bo

71. Kitchen

kitchen	부엌	bu-eok
gas	가스	ga-seu
gas cooker	가스 레인지	ga-seu re-in-ji
electric cooker	전기 레인지	jeon-gi re-in-ji
oven	오븐	o-beun
microwave oven	전자 레인지	jeon-ja re-in-ji
refrigerator	냉장고	naeng-jang-go
freezer	냉동고	naeng-dong-go
dishwasher	식기 세척기	sik-gi se-cheok-gi
mincer	고기 분쇄기	go-gi bun-swae-gi
juicer	과즙기	gwa-jeup-gi
toaster	토스터	to-seu-teo
mixer	믹서기	mik-seo-gi
coffee machine	커피 메이커	keo-pi me-i-keo
coffee pot	커피 주전자	keo-pi ju-jeon-ja
coffee grinder	커피 그라인더	keo-pi geu-ra-in-deo
kettle	주전자	ju-jeon-ja
teapot	티팟	ti-pat
lid	뚜껑	ttu-kkeong
tea strainer	차거름망	cha-geo-reum-mang
spoon	숟가락	sut-ga-rak
teaspoon	티스푼	ti-seu-pun
soup spoon	숟가락	sut-ga-rak
fork	포크	po-keu
knife	칼	kal

tableware (dishes)	식기	sik-gi
plate (dinner ~)	접시	jeop-si
saucer	받침 접시	bat-chim jeop-si
shot glass	소주잔	so-ju-jan
glass (tumbler)	유리잔	yu-ri-jan
cup	컵	keop
sugar bowl	설탕그릇	seol-tang-geu-reut
salt cellar	소금통	so-geum-tong
pepper pot	후추통	hu-chu-tong
butter dish	버터 접시	beo-teo jeop-si
stock pot (soup pot)	냄비	naem-bi
frying pan (skillet)	프라이팬	peu-ra-i-paen
ladle	국자	guk-ja
colander	체	che
tray (serving ~)	쟁반	jaeng-ban
bottle	병	byeong
jar (glass)	유리병	yu-ri-byeong
tin (can)	캔, 깡통	kaen, kkang-tong
bottle opener	병따개	byeong-tta-gae
tin opener	깡통 따개	kkang-tong tta-gae
corkscrew	코르크 마개 뽑이	ko-reu-keu ma-gae ppo-bi
filter	필터	pil-teo
to filter (vt)	여과하다	yeo-gwa-ha-da
waste (food ~, etc.)	쓰레기	sseu-re-gi
waste bin (kitchen ~)	쓰레기통	sseu-re-gi-tong

72. Bathroom

bathroom	욕실	yok-sil
water	물	mul
tap	수도꼭지	su-do-kkok-ji
hot water	온수	on-su
cold water	냉수	naeng-su
toothpaste	치약	chi-yak
to clean one's teeth	이를 닦다	i-reul dak-da
to shave (vi)	깎다	kkak-da
shaving foam	면도 크림	myeon-do keu-rim
razor	면도기	myeon-do-gi
to wash (one's hands, etc.)	씻다	ssit-da
to have a bath	목욕하다	mo-gyok-a-da
shower	샤워	sya-wo
to have a shower	샤워하다	sya-wo-ha-da
bath	욕조	yok-jo
toilet (toilet bowl)	변기	byeon-gi

sink (washbasin)	세면대	se-myeon-dae
soap	비누	bi-nu
soap dish	비누 그릇	bi-nu geu-reut
sponge	스펀지	seu-peon-ji
shampoo	샴푸	syam-pu
towel	수건	su-geon
bathrobe	목욕가운	mo-gyok-ga-un
laundry (laundering)	빨래	ppal-lae
washing machine	세탁기	se-tak-gi
to do the laundry	빨래하다	ppal-lae-ha-da
washing powder	가루세제	ga-ru-se-je

73. Household appliances

TV, telly	텔레비전	tel-le-bi-jeon
tape recorder	카세트 플레이어	ka-se-teu peul-le-i-eo
video	비디오테이프 녹화기	bi-di-o-te-i-peu nok-wa-gi
radio	라디오	ra-di-o
player (CD, MP3, etc.)	플레이어	peul-le-i-eo
video projector	프로젝터	peu-ro-jek-teo
home cinema	홈씨어터	hom-ssi-eo-teo
DVD player	디비디 플레이어	di-bi-di peul-le-i-eo
amplifier	앰프	aem-peu
video game console	게임기	ge-im-gi
video camera	캠코더	kaem-ko-deo
camera (photo)	카메라	ka-me-ra
digital camera	디지털 카메라	di-ji-teol ka-me-ra
vacuum cleaner	진공 청소기	jin-gong cheong-so-gi
iron (e.g. steam ~)	다리미	da-ri-mi
ironing board	다림질 판	da-rim-jil pan
telephone	전화	jeon-hwa
mobile phone	휴대폰	hyu-dae-pon
typewriter	타자기	ta-ja-gi
sewing machine	재봉틀	jae-bong-teul
microphone	마이크	ma-i-keu
headphones	헤드폰	he-deu-pon
remote control (TV)	원격 조종	won-gyeok jo-jong
CD, compact disc	씨디	ssi-di
cassette, tape	테이프	te-i-peu
vinyl record	레코드 판	re-ko-deu pan

THE EARTH. WEATHER

74. Outer space

space	우주	u-ju
space (as adj)	우주의	u-ju-ui
outer space	우주 공간	u-ju gong-gan
world	세계	se-gye
universe	우주	u-ju
galaxy	은하	eun-ha
star	별, 항성	byeol, hang-seong
constellation	별자리	byeol-ja-ri
planet	행성	haeng-seong
satellite	인공위성	in-gong-wi-seong
meteorite	운석	un-seok
comet	혜성	hye-seong
asteroid	소행성	so-haeng-seong
orbit	궤도	gwe-do
to revolve (~ around the Earth)	회전한다	hoe-jeon-han-da
atmosphere	대기	dae-gi
the Sun	태양	tae-yang
solar system	태양계	tae-yang-gye
solar eclipse	일식	il-sik
the Earth	지구	ji-gu
the Moon	달	dal
Mars	화성	hwa-seong
Venus	금성	geum-seong
Jupiter	목성	mok-seong
Saturn	토성	to-seong
Mercury	수성	su-seong
Uranus	천왕성	cheon-wang-seong
Neptune	해왕성	hae-wang-seong
Pluto	명왕성	myeong-wang-seong
Milky Way	은하수	eun-ha-su
Great Bear (Ursa Major)	큰곰자리	keun-gom-ja-ri
North Star	북극성	buk-geuk-seong
Martian	화성인	hwa-seong-in
extraterrestrial (n)	외계인	oe-gye-in
alien	외계인	oe-gye-in
flying saucer	비행 접시	bi-haeng jeop-si

| spaceship | 우주선 | u-ju-seon |
| space station | 우주 정거장 | u-ju jeong-nyu-jang |

engine	엔진	en-jin
nozzle	노즐	no-jeul
fuel	연료	yeol-lyo

cockpit, flight deck	조종석	jo-jong-seok
aerial	안테나	an-te-na
porthole	현창	hyeon-chang
solar panel	태양 전지	tae-yang jeon-ji
spacesuit	우주복	u-ju-bok

| weightlessness | 무중력 | mu-jung-nyeok |
| oxygen | 산소 | san-so |

| docking (in space) | 도킹 | do-king |
| to dock (vi, vt) | 도킹하다 | do-king-ha-da |

observatory	천문대	cheon-mun-dae
telescope	망원경	mang-won-gyeong
to observe (vt)	관찰하다	gwan-chal-ha-da
to explore (vt)	탐험하다	tam-heom-ha-da

75. The Earth

the Earth	지구	ji-gu
the globe (the Earth)	지구	ji-gu
planet	행성	haeng-seong
atmosphere	대기	dae-gi
geography	지리학	ji-ri-hak
nature	자연	ja-yeon

globe (table ~)	지구의	ji-gu-ui
map	지도	ji-do
atlas	지도첩	ji-do-cheop

Europe	유럽	yu-reop
Asia	아시아	a-si-a
Africa	아프리카	a-peu-ri-ka
Australia	호주	ho-ju

America	아메리카 대륙	a-me-ri-ka dae-ryuk
North America	북아메리카	bu-ga-me-ri-ka
South America	남아메리카	nam-a-me-ri-ka
Antarctica	남극 대륙	nam-geuk dae-ryuk
the Arctic	극지방	geuk-ji-bang

76. Cardinal directions

| north | 북쪽 | buk-jjok |
| to the north | 북쪽으로 | buk-jjo-geu-ro |

in the north	북쪽에	buk-jjo-ge
northern (adj)	북쪽의	buk-jjo-gui
south	남쪽	nam-jjok
to the south	남쪽으로	nam-jjo-geu-ro
in the south	남쪽에	nam-jjo-ge
southern (adj)	남쪽의	nam-jjo-gui
west	서쪽	seo-jjok
to the west	서쪽으로	seo-jjo-geu-ro
in the west	서쪽에	seo-jjo-ge
western (adj)	서쪽의	seo-jjo-gui
east	동쪽	dong-jjok
to the east	동쪽으로	dong-jjo-geu-ro
in the east	동쪽에	dong-jjo-ge
eastern (adj)	동쪽의	dong-jjo-gui

77. Sea. Ocean

sea	바다	ba-da
ocean	대양	dae-yang
gulf (bay)	만	man
straits	해협	hae-hyeop
continent (mainland)	대륙	dae-ryuk
island	섬	seom
peninsula	반도	ban-do
archipelago	군도	gun-do
bay, cove	만	man
harbour	항구	hang-gu
lagoon	석호	seok-o
cape	곶	got
atoll	환초	hwan-cho
reef	암초	am-cho
coral	산호	san-ho
coral reef	산호초	san-ho-cho
deep (adj)	깊은	gi-peun
depth (deep water)	깊이	gi-pi
trench (e.g. Mariana ~)	해구	hae-gu
current (Ocean ~)	해류	hae-ryu
to surround (bathe)	둘러싸다	dul-leo-ssa-da
shore	해변	hae-byeon
coast	바닷가	ba-dat-ga
flow (flood tide)	밀물	mil-mul
ebb (ebb tide)	썰물	sseol-mul
shoal	모래톱	mo-rae-top
bottom (~ of the sea)	해저	hae-jeo

wave	파도	pa-do
crest (~ of a wave)	물마루	mul-ma-ru
spume (sea foam)	거품	geo-pum

hurricane	허리케인	heo-ri-ke-in
tsunami	해일	hae-il
calm (dead ~)	고요함	go-yo-ham
quiet, calm (adj)	고요한	go-yo-han

| pole | 극 | geuk |
| polar (adj) | 극지의 | geuk-ji-ui |

latitude	위도	wi-do
longitude	경도	gyeong-do
parallel	위도선	wi-do-seon
equator	적도	jeok-do

sky	하늘	ha-neul
horizon	수평선	su-pyeong-seon
air	공기	gong-gi

lighthouse	등대	deung-dae
to dive (vi)	뛰어들다	ttwi-eo-deul-da
to sink (ab. boat)	가라앉다	ga-ra-an-da
treasure	보물	bo-mul

78. Seas & Oceans names

Atlantic Ocean	대서양	dae-seo-yang
Indian Ocean	인도양	in-do-yang
Pacific Ocean	태평양	tae-pyeong-yang
Arctic Ocean	북극해	buk-geuk-ae

Black Sea	흑해	heuk-ae
Red Sea	홍해	hong-hae
Yellow Sea	황해	hwang-hae
White Sea	백해	baek-ae

Caspian Sea	카스피 해	ka-seu-pi hae
Dead Sea	사해	sa-hae
Mediterranean Sea	지중해	ji-jung-hae

| Aegean Sea | 에게 해 | e-ge hae |
| Adriatic Sea | 아드리아 해 | a-deu-ri-a hae |

Arabian Sea	아라비아 해	a-ra-bi-a hae
Sea of Japan	동해	dong-hae
Bering Sea	베링 해	be-ring hae
South China Sea	남중국해	nam-jung-guk-ae

Coral Sea	산호해	san-ho-hae
Tasman Sea	태즈먼 해	tae-jeu-meon hae
Caribbean Sea	카리브 해	ka-ri-beu hae
Barents Sea	바렌츠 해	ba-ren-cheu hae

Kara Sea	카라 해	ka-ra hae
North Sea	북해	buk-ae
Baltic Sea	발트 해	bal-teu hae
Norwegian Sea	노르웨이 해	no-reu-we-i hae

79. Mountains

mountain	산	san
mountain range	산맥	san-maek
mountain ridge	능선	neung-seon
summit, top	정상	jeong-sang
peak	봉우리	bong-u-ri
foot (~ of the mountain)	기슭	gi-seuk
slope (mountainside)	경사면	gyeong-sa-myeon
volcano	화산	hwa-san
active volcano	활화산	hwal-hwa-san
dormant volcano	사화산	sa-hwa-san
eruption	폭발	pok-bal
crater	분화구	bun-hwa-gu
magma	마그마	ma-geu-ma
lava	용암	yong-am
molten (~ lava)	녹은	no-geun
canyon	협곡	hyeop-gok
gorge	협곡	hyeop-gok
crevice	갈라진	gal-la-jin
pass, col	산길	san-gil
plateau	고원	go-won
cliff	절벽	jeol-byeok
hill	언덕, 작은 산	eon-deok, ja-geun san
glacier	빙하	bing-ha
waterfall	폭포	pok-po
geyser	간헐천	gan-heol-cheon
lake	호수	ho-su
plain	평원	pyeong-won
landscape	경관	gyeong-gwan
echo	메아리	me-a-ri
alpinist	등산가	deung-san-ga
rock climber	암벽 등반가	am-byeok deung-ban-ga
to conquer (in climbing)	정복하다	jeong-bok-a-da
climb (an easy ~)	등반	deung-ban

80. Mountains names

The Alps	알프스 산맥	al-peu-seu san-maek
Mont Blanc	몽블랑 산	mong-beul-lang san

The Pyrenees	피레네 산맥	pi-re-ne san-maek
The Carpathians	카르파티아 산맥	ka-reu-pa-ti-a san-maek
The Ural Mountains	우랄 산맥	u-ral san-maek
The Caucasus Mountains	코카서스 산맥	ko-ka-seo-seu san-maek
Mount Elbrus	엘브루스 산	el-beu-ru-seu san
The Altai Mountains	알타이 산맥	al-ta-i san-maek
The Tian Shan	톈샨 산맥	ten-syan san-maek
The Pamirs	파미르 고원	pa-mi-reu go-won
The Himalayas	히말라야 산맥	hi-mal-la-ya san-maek
Mount Everest	에베레스트 산	e-be-re-seu-teu san
The Andes	안데스 산맥	an-de-seu san-maek
Mount Kilimanjaro	킬리만자로 산	kil-li-man-ja-ro san

81. Rivers

river	강	gang
spring (natural source)	샘	saem
riverbed (river channel)	강바닥	gang-ba-dak
basin (river valley)	유역	yu-yeok
to flow into ...	··· 로 흘러가다	... ro heul-leo-ga-da
tributary	지류	ji-ryu
bank (river ~)	둑	duk
current (stream)	흐름	heu-reum
downstream (adv)	하류로	gang ha-ryu-ro
upstream (adv)	상류로	sang-nyu-ro
inundation	홍수	hong-su
flooding	홍수	hong-su
to overflow (vi)	범람하다	beom-nam-ha-da
to flood (vt)	범람하다	beom-nam-ha-da
shallow (shoal)	얕은 곳	ya-teun got
rapids	여울	yeo-ul
dam	댐	daem
canal	운하	un-ha
reservoir (artificial lake)	저수지	jeo-su-ji
sluice, lock	수문	su-mun
water body (pond, etc.)	저장 수량	jeo-jang su-ryang
swamp (marshland)	늪, 소택지	neup, so-taek-ji
bog, marsh	수렁	su-reong
whirlpool	소용돌이	so-yong-do-ri
stream (brook)	개울, 시내	gae-ul, si-nae
drinking (ab. water)	마실 수 있는	ma-sil su in-neun
fresh (~ water)	민물의	min-mu-rui
ice	얼음	eo-reum
to freeze over (ab. river, etc.)	얼다	eol-da

82. Rivers names

Seine	센 강	sen gang
Loire	루아르 강	ru-a-reu gang
Thames	템스 강	tem-seu gang
Rhine	라인 강	ra-in gang
Danube	도나우 강	do-na-u gang
Volga	볼가 강	bol-ga gang
Don	돈 강	don gang
Lena	레나 강	re-na gang
Yellow River	황허강	hwang-heo-gang
Yangtze	양자강	yang-ja-gang
Mekong	메콩 강	me-kong gang
Ganges	갠지스 강	gaen-ji-seu gang
Nile River	나일 강	na-il gang
Congo River	콩고 강	kong-go gang
Okavango River	오카방고 강	o-ka-bang-go gang
Zambezi River	잠베지 강	jam-be-ji gang
Limpopo River	림포포 강	rim-po-po gang

83. Forest

forest, wood	숲	sup
forest (as adj)	산림의	sal-li-mui
thick forest	밀림	mil-lim
grove	작은 숲	ja-geun sup
forest clearing	빈터	bin-teo
thicket	덤불	deom-bul
scrubland	관목지	gwan-mok-ji
footpath (troddenpath)	오솔길	o-sol-gil
gully	도랑	do-rang
tree	나무	na-mu
leaf	잎	ip
leaves (foliage)	나뭇잎	na-mun-nip
fall of leaves	낙엽	na-gyeop
to fall (ab. leaves)	떨어지다	tteo-reo-ji-da
branch	가지	ga-ji
bough	큰 가지	keun ga-ji
bud (on shrub, tree)	잎눈	im-nun
needle (of the pine tree)	바늘	ba-neul
fir cone	솔방울	sol-bang-ul
tree hollow	구멍	gu-meong
nest	둥지	dung-ji

burrow (animal hole)	굴	gul
trunk	몸통	mom-tong
root	뿌리	ppu-ri
bark	껍질	kkeop-jil
moss	이끼	i-kki
to uproot (remove trees or tree stumps)	수목을 통제 뽑다	su-mo-geul tong-jjae ppop-da
to chop down	자르다	ja-reu-da
to deforest (vt)	삼림을 없애다	sam-ni-meul reop-sae-da
tree stump	그루터기	geu-ru-teo-gi
campfire	모닥불	mo-dak-bul
forest fire	산불	san-bul
to extinguish (vt)	끄다	kkeu-da
forest ranger	산림경비원	sal-lim-gyeong-bi-won
protection	보호	bo-ho
to protect (~ nature)	보호하다	bo-ho-ha-da
poacher	밀렵자	mil-lyeop-ja
steel trap	덫	deot
to gather, to pick (vt)	따다	tta-da
to lose one's way	길을 잃다	gi-reul ril-ta

84. Natural resources

natural resources	천연 자원	cheo-nyeon ja-won
deposits	매장량	mae-jang-nyang
field (e.g. oilfield)	지역	ji-yeok
to mine (extract)	채광하다	chae-gwang-ha-da
mining (extraction)	막장일	mak-jang-il
ore	광석	gwang-seok
mine (e.g. for coal)	광산	gwang-san
shaft (mine ~)	갱도	gaeng-do
miner	광부	gwang-bu
gas (natural ~)	가스	ga-seu
gas pipeline	가스관	ga-seu-gwan
oil (petroleum)	석유	seo-gyu
oil pipeline	석유 파이프라인	seo-gyu pa-i-peu-ra-in
oil well	유정	yu-jeong
derrick (tower)	유정탑	yu-jeong-tap
tanker	유조선	yu-jo-seon
sand	모래	mo-rae
limestone	석회석	seok-oe-seok
gravel	자갈	ja-gal
peat	토탄	to-tan
clay	점토	jeom-to
coal	석탄	seok-tan
iron (ore)	철	cheol

gold	금	geum
silver	은	eun
nickel	니켈	ni-kel
copper	구리	gu-ri
zinc	아연	a-yeon
manganese	망간	mang-gan
mercury	수은	su-eun
lead	납	nap
mineral	광물	gwang-mul
crystal	수정	su-jeong
marble	대리석	dae-ri-seok
uranium	우라늄	u-ra-nyum

85. Weather

weather	날씨	nal-ssi
weather forecast	일기 예보	il-gi ye-bo
temperature	온도	on-do
thermometer	온도계	on-do-gye
barometer	기압계	gi-ap-gye
humidity	습함, 습기	seu-pam, seup-gi
heat (extreme ~)	더위	deo-wi
hot (torrid)	더운	deo-un
it's hot	덥다	deop-da
it's warm	따뜻하다	tta-tteu-ta-da
warm (moderately hot)	따뜻한	tta-tteu-tan
it's cold	춥다	chup-da
cold (adj)	추운	chu-un
sun	해	hae
to shine (vi)	빛나다	bin-na-da
sunny (day)	화창한	hwa-chang-han
to come up (vi)	뜨다	tteu-da
to set (vi)	지다	ji-da
cloud	구름	gu-reum
cloudy (adj)	구름의	gu-reum-ui
somber (gloomy)	흐린	heu-rin
rain	비	bi
it's raining	비가 오다	bi-ga o-da
rainy (~ day, weather)	비가 오는	bi-ga o-neun
to drizzle (vi)	이슬비가 내리다	i-seul-bi-ga nae-ri-da
pouring rain	억수	eok-su
downpour	호우	ho-u
heavy (e.g. ~ rain)	심한	sim-han
puddle	웅덩이	ung-deong-i
to get wet (in rain)	젖다	jeot-da

fog (mist)	안개	an-gae
foggy	안개가 자욱한	an-gae-ga ja-uk-an
snow	눈	nun
it's snowing	눈이 오다	nun-i o-da

86. Severe weather. Natural disasters

thunderstorm	뇌우	noe-u
lightning (~ strike)	번개	beon-gae
to flash (vi)	번쩍이다	beon-jjeo-gi-da

thunder	천둥	cheon-dung
to thunder (vi)	천둥이 치다	cheon-dung-i chi-da
it's thundering	천둥이 치다	cheon-dung-i chi-da

| hail | 싸락눈 | ssa-rang-nun |
| it's hailing | 싸락눈이 내리다 | ssa-rang-nun-i nae-ri-da |

| to flood (vt) | 범람하다 | beom-nam-ha-da |
| flood, inundation | 홍수 | hong-su |

earthquake	지진	ji-jin
tremor, shoke	진동	jin-dong
epicentre	진앙	jin-ang

| eruption | 폭발 | pok-bal |
| lava | 용암 | yong-am |

twister	회오리바람	hoe-o-ri-ba-ram
tornado	토네이도	to-ne-i-do
typhoon	태풍	tae-pung

hurricane	허리케인	heo-ri-ke-in
storm	폭풍우	pok-pung-u
tsunami	해일	hae-il

fire (accident)	불	bul
disaster	재해	jae-hae
meteorite	운석	un-seok

avalanche	눈사태	nun-sa-tae
snowslide	눈사태	nun-sa-tae
blizzard	눈보라	nun-bo-ra
snowstorm	눈보라	nun-bo-ra

FAUNA

87. Mammals. Predators

predator	육식 동물	yuk-sik dong-mul
tiger	호랑이	ho-rang-i
lion	사자	sa-ja
wolf	이리	i-ri
fox	여우	yeo-u

jaguar	재규어	jae-gyu-eo
leopard	표범	pyo-beom
cheetah	치타	chi-ta

puma	퓨마	pyu-ma
snow leopard	눈표범	nun-pyo-beom
lynx	스라소니	seu-ra-so-ni

coyote	코요테	ko-yo-te
jackal	재칼	jae-kal
hyena	하이에나	ha-i-e-na

88. Wild animals

animal	동물	dong-mul
beast (animal)	짐승	jim-seung

squirrel	다람쥐	da-ram-jwi
hedgehog	고슴도치	go-seum-do-chi
hare	토끼	to-kki
rabbit	굴토끼	gul-to-kki

badger	오소리	o-so-ri
raccoon	너구리	neo-gu-ri
hamster	햄스터	haem-seu-teo
marmot	마멋	ma-meot

mole	두더지	du-deo-ji
mouse	생쥐	saeng-jwi
rat	시궁쥐	si-gung-jwi
bat	박쥐	bak-jwi

ermine	북방족제비	buk-bang-jok-je-bi
sable	검은담비	geo-meun-dam-bi
marten	담비	dam-bi
mink	밍크	ming-keu
beaver	비버	bi-beo
otter	수달	su-dal

horse	말	mal
moose	엘크, 무스	el-keu, mu-seu
deer	사슴	sa-seum
camel	낙타	nak-ta
bison	미국들소	mi-guk-deul-so
wisent	유럽들소	yu-reop-deul-so
buffalo	물소	mul-so
zebra	얼룩말	eol-lung-mal
antelope	영양	yeong-yang
roe deer	노루	no-ru
fallow deer	다마사슴	da-ma-sa-seum
chamois	샤모아	sya-mo-a
wild boar	멧돼지	met-dwae-ji
whale	고래	go-rae
seal	바다표범	ba-da-pyo-beom
walrus	바다코끼리	ba-da-ko-kki-ri
fur seal	물개	mul-gae
dolphin	돌고래	dol-go-rae
bear	곰	gom
polar bear	북극곰	buk-geuk-gom
panda	판다	pan-da
monkey	원숭이	won-sung-i
chimpanzee	침팬지	chim-paen-ji
orangutan	오랑우탄	o-rang-u-tan
gorilla	고릴라	go-ril-la
macaque	마카크	ma-ka-keu
gibbon	긴팔원숭이	gin-pa-rwon-sung-i
elephant	코끼리	ko-kki-ri
rhinoceros	코뿔소	ko-ppul-so
giraffe	기린	gi-rin
hippopotamus	하마	ha-ma
kangaroo	캥거루	kaeng-geo-ru
koala (bear)	코알라	ko-al-la
mongoose	몽구스	mong-gu-seu
chinchilla	친칠라	chin-chil-la
skunk	스컹크	seu-keong-keu
porcupine	호저	ho-jeo

89. Domestic animals

cat	고양이	go-yang-i
tomcat	수고양이	su-go-yang-i
horse	말	mal
stallion (male horse)	수말, 종마	su-mal, jong-ma
mare	암말	am-mal

cow	암소	am-so
bull	황소	hwang-so
ox	수소	su-so
sheep (ewe)	양, 암양	yang, a-myang
ram	수양	su-yang
goat	염소	yeom-so
billy goat, he-goat	숫염소	sun-nyeom-so
donkey	당나귀	dang-na-gwi
mule	노새	no-sae
pig	돼지	dwae-ji
piglet	돼지 새끼	dwae-ji sae-kki
rabbit	집토끼	jip-to-kki
hen (chicken)	암탉	am-tak
cock	수탉	su-tak
duck	집오리	ji-bo-ri
drake	수오리	su-o-ri
goose	집거위	jip-geo-wi
tom turkey, gobbler	수칠면조	su-chil-myeon-jo
turkey (hen)	칠면조	chil-myeon-jo
domestic animals	가축	ga-chuk
tame (e.g. ~ hamster)	길들여진	gil-deu-ryeo-jin
to tame (vt)	길들이다	gil-deu-ri-da
to breed (vt)	사육하다, 기르다	sa-yuk-a-da, gi-reu-da
farm	농장	nong-jang
poultry	가금	ga-geum
cattle	가축	ga-chuk
herd (cattle)	떼	tte
stable	마구간	ma-gu-gan
pigsty	돼지 우리	dwae-ji u-ri
cowshed	외양간	oe-yang-gan
rabbit hutch	토끼장	to-kki-jang
hen house	닭장	dak-jang

90. Birds

bird	새	sae
pigeon	비둘기	bi-dul-gi
sparrow	참새	cham-sae
tit (great tit)	박새	bak-sae
magpie	까치	kka-chi
raven	갈가마귀	gal-ga-ma-gwi
crow	까마귀	kka-ma-gwi
jackdaw	갈가마귀	gal-ga-ma-gwi
rook	떼까마귀	ttae-kka-ma-gwi

duck	오리	o-ri
goose	거위	geo-wi
pheasant	꿩	kkwong
eagle	독수리	dok-su-ri
hawk	매	mae
falcon	매	mae
vulture	독수리, 콘도르	dok-su-ri, kon-do-reu
condor (Andean ~)	콘도르	kon-do-reu
swan	백조	baek-jo
crane	두루미	du-ru-mi
stork	황새	hwang-sae
parrot	앵무새	aeng-mu-sae
hummingbird	벌새	beol-sae
peacock	공작	gong-jak
ostrich	타조	ta-jo
heron	왜가리	wae-ga-ri
flamingo	플라밍고	peul-la-ming-go
pelican	펠리컨	pel-li-keon
nightingale	나이팅게일	na-i-ting-ge-il
swallow	제비	je-bi
thrush	지빠귀	ji-ppa-gwi
song thrush	노래지빠귀	no-rae-ji-ppa-gwi
blackbird	대륙검은지빠귀	dae-ryuk-geo-meun-ji-ppa-gwi
swift	칼새	kal-sae
lark	종다리	jong-da-ri
quail	메추라기	me-chu-ra-gi
woodpecker	딱따구리	ttak-tta-gu-ri
cuckoo	뻐꾸기	ppeo-kku-gi
owl	올빼미	ol-ppae-mi
eagle owl	수리부엉이	su-ri-bu-eong-i
wood grouse	큰뇌조	keun-noe-jo
black grouse	멧닭	met-dak
partridge	자고	ja-go
starling	찌르레기	jji-reu-re-gi
canary	카나리아	ka-na-ri-a
chaffinch	되새	doe-sae
bullfinch	피리새	pi-ri-sae
seagull	갈매기	gal-mae-gi
albatross	신천옹	sin-cheon-ong
penguin	펭귄	peng-gwin

91. Fish. Marine animals

bream	도미류	do-mi-ryu
carp	잉어	ing-eo

perch	농어의 일종	nong-eo-ui il-jong
catfish	메기	me-gi
pike	북부민물꼬치고기	buk-bu-min-mul-kko-chi-go-gi
salmon	연어	yeon-eo
sturgeon	철갑상어	cheol-gap-sang-eo
herring	청어	cheong-eo
Atlantic salmon	대서양 연어	dae-seo-yang yeon-eo
mackerel	고등어	go-deung-eo
flatfish	넙치	neop-chi
cod	대구	dae-gu
tuna	참치	cham-chi
trout	송어	song-eo
eel	뱀장어	baem-jang-eo
electric ray	시끈가오리	si-kkeun-ga-o-ri
moray eel	곰치	gom-chi
piranha	피라니아	pi-ra-ni-a
shark	상어	sang-eo
dolphin	돌고래	dol-go-rae
whale	고래	go-rae
crab	게	ge
jellyfish	해파리	hae-pa-ri
octopus	낙지	nak-ji
starfish	불가사리	bul-ga-sa-ri
sea urchin	성게	seong-ge
seahorse	해마	hae-ma
oyster	굴	gul
prawn	새우	sae-u
lobster	바닷가재	ba-dat-ga-jae
spiny lobster	대하	dae-ha

92. Amphibians. Reptiles

snake	뱀	baem
venomous (snake)	독이 있는	do-gi in-neun
viper	살무사	sal-mu-sa
cobra	코브라	ko-beu-ra
python	비단뱀	bi-dan-baem
boa	보아	bo-a
grass snake	풀뱀	pul-baem
rattle snake	방울뱀	bang-ul-baem
anaconda	아나콘다	a-na-kon-da
lizard	도마뱀	do-ma-baem
iguana	이구아나	i-gu-a-na

salamander	도롱뇽	do-rong-nyong
chameleon	카멜레온	ka-mel-le-on
scorpion	전갈	jeon-gal
turtle	거북	geo-buk
frog	개구리	gae-gu-ri
toad	두꺼비	du-kkeo-bi
crocodile	악어	a-geo

93. Insects

insect	곤충	gon-chung
butterfly	나비	na-bi
ant	개미	gae-mi
fly	파리	pa-ri
mosquito	모기	mo-gi
beetle	딱정벌레	ttak-jeong-beol-le
wasp	말벌	mal-beol
bee	꿀벌	kkul-beol
bumblebee	호박벌	ho-bak-beol
gadfly (botfly)	쇠파리	soe-pa-ri
spider	거미	geo-mi
spider's web	거미줄	geo-mi-jul
dragonfly	잠자리	jam-ja-ri
grasshopper	메뚜기	me-ttu-gi
moth (night butterfly)	나방	na-bang
cockroach	바퀴벌레	ba-kwi-beol-le
tick	진드기	jin-deu-gi
flea	벼룩	byeo-ruk
midge	깔따구	kkal-tta-gu
locust	메뚜기	me-ttu-gi
snail	달팽이	dal-paeng-i
cricket	귀뚜라미	gwi-ttu-ra-mi
firefly	개똥벌레	gae-ttong-beol-le
ladybird	무당벌레	mu-dang-beol-le
cockchafer	왕풍뎅이	wang-pung-deng-i
leech	거머리	geo-meo-ri
caterpillar	애벌레	ae-beol-le
earthworm	지렁이	ji-reong-i
larva	애벌레	ae-beol-le

FLORA

tree	나무	na-mu
deciduous (adj)	낙엽수의	na-gyeop-su-ui
coniferous (adj)	침엽수의	chi-myeop-su-ui
evergreen (adj)	상록의	sang-no-gui
apple tree	사과나무	sa-gwa-na-mu
pear tree	배나무	bae-na-mu
cherry tree	벚나무	beon-na-mu
plum tree	자두나무	ja-du-na-mu
birch	자작나무	ja-jang-na-mu
oak	오크	o-keu
linden tree	보리수	bo-ri-su
aspen	사시나무	sa-si-na-mu
maple	단풍나무	dan-pung-na-mu
spruce	가문비나무	ga-mun-bi-na-mu
pine	소나무	so-na-mu
larch	낙엽송	na-gyeop-song
fir tree	전나무	jeon-na-mu
cedar	시다	si-da
poplar	포플러	po-peul-leo
rowan	마가목	ma-ga-mok
willow	버드나무	beo-deu-na-mu
alder	오리나무	o-ri-na-mu
beech	너도밤나무	neo-do-bam-na-mu
elm	느릅나무	neu-reum-na-mu
ash (tree)	물푸레나무	mul-pu-re-na-mu
chestnut	밤나무	bam-na-mu
magnolia	목련	mong-nyeon
palm tree	야자나무	ya-ja-na-mu
cypress	사이프러스	sa-i-peu-reo-seu
mangrove	맹그로브	maeng-geu-ro-beu
baobab	바오밥나무	ba-o-bam-na-mu
eucalyptus	유칼립투스	yu-kal-lip-tu-seu
sequoia	세쿼이아	se-kwo-i-a

bush	덤불	deom-bul
shrub	관목	gwan-mok

grapevine	포도 덩굴	po-do deong-gul
vineyard	포도밭	po-do-bat
raspberry bush	라즈베리	ra-jeu-be-ri
redcurrant bush	레드커런트 나무	re-deu-keo-reon-teu na-mu
gooseberry bush	구스베리 나무	gu-seu-be-ri na-mu
acacia	아카시아	a-ka-si-a
barberry	매자나무	mae-ja-na-mu
jasmine	재스민	jae-seu-min
juniper	두송	du-song
rosebush	장미 덤불	jang-mi deom-bul
dog rose	찔레나무	jjil-le-na-mu

96. Fruits. Berries

apple	사과	sa-gwa
pear	배	bae
plum	자두	ja-du
strawberry (garden ~)	딸기	ttal-gi
sour cherry	신양	si-nyang
sweet cherry	양벚나무	yang-beon-na-mu
grape	포도	po-do
raspberry	라즈베리	ra-jeu-be-ri
blackcurrant	블랙커렌트	beul-laek-keo-ren-teu
redcurrant	레드커렌트	re-deu-keo-ren-teu
gooseberry	구스베리	gu-seu-be-ri
cranberry	크랜베리	keu-raen-be-ri
orange	오렌지	o-ren-ji
tangerine	귤	gyul
pineapple	파인애플	pa-in-ae-peul
banana	바나나	ba-na-na
date	대추야자	dae-chu-ya-ja
lemon	레몬	re-mon
apricot	살구	sal-gu
peach	복숭아	bok-sung-a
kiwi	키위	ki-wi
grapefruit	자몽	ja-mong
berry	장과	jang-gwa
berries	장과류	jang-gwa-ryu
cowberry	월귤나무	wol-gyul-la-mu
wild strawberry	야생딸기	ya-saeng-ttal-gi
bilberry	빌베리	bil-be-ri

97. Flowers. Plants

flower	꽃	kkot
bouquet (of flowers)	꽃다발	kkot-da-bal

rose (flower)	장미	jang-mi
tulip	튤립	tyul-lip
carnation	카네이션	ka-ne-i-syeon
gladiolus	글라디올러스	geul-la-di-ol-leo-seu

cornflower	수레국화	su-re-guk-wa
harebell	실잔대	sil-jan-dae
dandelion	민들레	min-deul-le
camomile	캐모마일	kae-mo-ma-il

aloe	알로에	al-lo-e
cactus	선인장	seon-in-jang
rubber plant, ficus	고무나무	go-mu-na-mu

lily	백합	baek-ap
geranium	제라늄	je-ra-nyum
hyacinth	히아신스	hi-a-sin-seu

mimosa	미모사	mi-mo-sa
narcissus	수선화	su-seon-hwa
nasturtium	한련	hal-lyeon

orchid	난초	nan-cho
peony	모란	mo-ran
violet	바이올렛	ba-i-ol-let

pansy	팬지	paen-ji
forget-me-not	물망초	mul-mang-cho
daisy	데이지	de-i-ji

poppy	양귀비	yang-gwi-bi
hemp	삼	sam
mint	박하	bak-a

| lily of the valley | 은방울꽃 | eun-bang-ul-kkot |
| snowdrop | 스노드롭 | seu-no-deu-rop |

nettle	쐐기풀	sswae-gi-pul
sorrel	수영	su-yeong
water lily	수련	su-ryeon
fern	고사리	go-sa-ri
lichen	이끼	i-kki

conservatory (greenhouse)	온실	on-sil
lawn	잔디	jan-di
flowerbed	꽃밭	kkot-bat

plant	식물	sing-mul
grass	풀	pul
blade of grass	풀잎	pu-rip

leaf	잎	ip
petal	꽃잎	kko-chip
stem	줄기	jul-gi
tuber	구근	gu-geun
young plant (shoot)	새싹	sae-ssak

thorn	가시	ga-si
to blossom (vi)	피우다	pi-u-da
to fade, to wither	시들다	si-deul-da
smell (odour)	향기	hyang-gi
to cut (flowers)	자르다	ja-reu-da
to pick (a flower)	따다	tta-da

98. Cereals, grains

grain	곡물	gong-mul
cereal crops	곡류	gong-nyu
ear (of barley, etc.)	이삭	i-sak
wheat	밀	mil
rye	호밀	ho-mil
oats	귀리	gwi-ri
millet	수수, 기장	su-su, gi-jang
barley	보리	bo-ri
maize	옥수수	ok-su-su
rice	쌀	ssal
buckwheat	메밀	me-mil
pea plant	완두	wan-du
kidney bean	강낭콩	gang-nang-kong
soya	콩	kong
lentil	렌즈콩	ren-jeu-kong
beans (pulse crops)	콩	kong

COUNTRIES OF THE WORLD

99. Countries. Part 1

Afghanistan	아프가니스탄	a-peu-ga-ni-seu-tan
Albania	알바니아	al-ba-ni-a
Argentina	아르헨티나	a-reu-hen-ti-na
Armenia	아르메니아	a-reu-me-ni-a
Australia	호주	ho-ju
Austria	오스트리아	o-seu-teu-ri-a
Azerbaijan	아제르바이잔	a-je-reu-ba-i-jan
The Bahamas	바하마	ba-ha-ma
Bangladesh	방글라데시	bang-geul-la-de-si
Belarus	벨로루시	bel-lo-ru-si
Belgium	벨기에	bel-gi-e
Bolivia	볼리비아	bol-li-bi-a
Bosnia and Herzegovina	보스니아 헤르체코비나	bo-seu-ni-a he-reu-che-ko-bi-na
Brazil	브라질	beu-ra-jil
Bulgaria	불가리아	bul-ga-ri-a
Cambodia	캄보디아	kam-bo-di-a
Canada	캐나다	kae-na-da
Chile	칠레	chil-le
China	중국	jung-guk
Colombia	콜롬비아	kol-lom-bi-a
Croatia	크로아티아	keu-ro-a-ti-a
Cuba	쿠바	ku-ba
Cyprus	키프로스	ki-peu-ro-seu
Czech Republic	체코	che-ko
Denmark	덴마크	den-ma-keu
Dominican Republic	도미니카 공화국	do-mi-ni-ka gong-hwa-guk
Ecuador	에콰도르	e-kwa-do-reu
Egypt	이집트	i-jip-teu
England	잉글랜드	ing-geul-laen-deu
Estonia	에스토니아	e-seu-to-ni-a
Finland	핀란드	pil-lan-deu
France	프랑스	peu-rang-seu
French Polynesia	폴리네시아	pol-li-ne-si-a
Georgia	그루지야	geu-ru-ji-ya
Germany	독일	do-gil
Ghana	가나	ga-na
Great Britain	영국	yeong-guk
Greece	그리스	geu-ri-seu
Haiti	아이티	a-i-ti
Hungary	헝가리	heong-ga-ri

100. Countries. Part 2

Iceland	아이슬란드	a-i-seul-lan-deu
India	인도	in-do
Indonesia	인도네시아	in-do-ne-si-a
Iran	이란	i-ran
Iraq	이라크	i-ra-keu
Ireland	아일랜드	a-il-laen-deu
Israel	이스라엘	i-seu-ra-el
Italy	이탈리아	i-tal-li-a
Jamaica	자메이카	ja-me-i-ka
Japan	일본	il-bon
Jordan	요르단	yo-reu-dan
Kazakhstan	카자흐스탄	ka-ja-heu-seu-tan
Kenya	케냐	ke-nya
Kirghizia	키르기스스탄	ki-reu-gi-seu-seu-tan
Kuwait	쿠웨이트	ku-we-i-teu
Laos	라오스	ra-o-seu
Latvia	라트비아	ra-teu-bi-a
Lebanon	레바논	re-ba-non
Libya	리비아	ri-bi-a
Liechtenstein	리히텐슈타인	ri-hi-ten-syu-ta-in
Lithuania	리투아니아	ri-tu-a-ni-a
Luxembourg	룩셈부르크	ruk-sem-bu-reu-keu
North Macedonia	마케도니아	ma-ke-do-ni-a
Madagascar	마다가스카르	ma-da-ga-seu-ka-reu
Malaysia	말레이시아	mal-le-i-si-a
Malta	몰타	mol-ta
Mexico	멕시코	mek-si-ko
Moldova, Moldavia	몰도바	mol-do-ba
Monaco	모나코	mo-na-ko
Mongolia	몽골	mong-gol
Montenegro	몬테네그로	mon-te-ne-geu-ro
Morocco	모로코	mo-ro-ko
Myanmar	미얀마	mi-yan-ma
Namibia	나미비아	na-mi-bi-a
Nepal	네팔	ne-pal
Netherlands	네덜란드	ne-deol-lan-deu
New Zealand	뉴질랜드	nyu-jil-laen-deu
North Korea	북한	buk-an
Norway	노르웨이	no-reu-we-i

101. Countries. Part 3

Pakistan	파키스탄	pa-ki-seu-tan
Palestine	팔레스타인	pal-le-seu-ta-in
Panama	파나마	pa-na-ma
Paraguay	파라과이	pa-ra-gwa-i

Peru	페루	pe-ru
Poland	폴란드	pol-lan-deu
Portugal	포르투갈	po-reu-tu-gal
Romania	루마니아	ru-ma-ni-a
Russia	러시아	reo-si-a

Saudi Arabia	사우디아라비아	sa-u-di-a-ra-bi-a
Scotland	스코틀랜드	seu-ko-teul-laen-deu
Senegal	세네갈	se-ne-gal
Serbia	세르비아	se-reu-bi-a
Slovakia	슬로바키아	seul-lo-ba-ki-a
Slovenia	슬로베니아	seul-lo-be-ni-a

South Africa	남아프리카 공화국	nam-a-peu-ri-ka gong-hwa-guk
South Korea	한국	han-guk
Spain	스페인	seu-pe-in
Suriname	수리남	su-ri-nam
Sweden	스웨덴	seu-we-den
Switzerland	스위스	seu-wi-seu
Syria	시리아	si-ri-a

Taiwan	대만	dae-man
Tajikistan	타지키스탄	ta-ji-ki-seu-tan
Tanzania	탄자니아	tan-ja-ni-a
Tasmania	태즈메이니아	tae-jeu-me-i-ni-a
Thailand	태국	tae-guk
Tunisia	튀니지	twi-ni-ji
Turkey	터키	teo-ki
Turkmenistan	투르크메니스탄	tu-reu-keu-me-ni-seu-tan

Ukraine	우크라이나	u-keu-ra-i-na
United Arab Emirates	아랍에미리트	a-ra-be-mi-ri-teu
United States of America	미국	mi-guk
Uruguay	우루과이	u-ru-gwa-i
Uzbekistan	우즈베키스탄	u-jeu-be-ki-seu-tan

Vatican City	바티칸	ba-ti-kan
Venezuela	베네수엘라	be-ne-su-el-la
Vietnam	베트남	be-teu-nam
Zanzibar	잔지바르	jan-ji-ba-reu

www.ingramcontent.com/pod-product-compliance
Lightning Source LLC
Chambersburg PA
CBHW070822050426
42452CB00011B/2154